Jennifer Lawrence

by Gail B. Stewart

LUCENT BOOKS
A part of Gale, Cengage Learning

GALE
CENGAGE Learning·

Farmington Hills, Mich • San Francisco • New York • Waterville, Maine
Meriden, Conn • Mason, Ohio • Chicago

GALE
CENGAGE Learning

LIBRARY OF CONGRESS CATALOGING-IN-PUBLICATION DATA

Stewart, Gail B. (Gail Barbara), 1949-
    Jennifer Lawrence / by Gail B. Stewart.
        pages cm -- (People in the news)
    Includes bibliographical references and index.
    ISBN 978-1-4205-1223-6 (hardback)
    1. Lawrence, Jennifer, 1990---Juvenile literature. 2. Actors--United
States--Biography--Juvenile literature. I. Title.
    PN2287.L28948S74 2015
    791.4302'8092--dc23
    [B]
                                    2014047760

Lucent Books
27500 Drake Rd.
Farmington Hills, MI 48331

ISBN-13: 978-1-4205-1223-6

Printed in the United States of America
1 2 3 4 5 6 7 19 18 17 16 15

Contents

Fame and celebrity are alluring. People are drawn to those who walk in fame's spotlight, whether they are known for great accomplishments or for notorious deeds. The lives of the famous pique public interest and attract attention, perhaps because their experiences seem in some ways so different from, yet in other ways so similar to, our own.

Newspapers, magazines, and television regularly capitalize on this fascination with celebrity by running profiles of famous people. For example, television programs such as *Entertainment Tonight* devote all their programming to stories about entertainment and entertainers. Magazines such as *People* fill their pages with stories of the private lives of famous people. Even newspapers, newsmagazines, and television news frequently delve into the lives of well-known personalities. Despite the number of articles and programs, few provide more than a superficial glimpse at their subjects.

Lucent's People in the News series offers young readers a deeper look into the lives of today's newsmakers, the influences that have shaped them, and the impact they have had in their fields of endeavor and on other people's lives. The subjects of the series hail from many disciplines and walks of life. They include authors, musicians, athletes, political leaders, entertainers, entrepreneurs, and others who have made a mark on modern life and who, in many cases, will continue to do so for years to come.

These biographies are more than factual chronicles. Each book emphasizes the contributions, accomplishments, or deeds that have brought fame or notoriety to the individual and shows how that person has influenced modern life. Authors portray their subjects in a realistic, unsentimental light. For example, Bill Gates—cofounder of the software giant Microsoft—has been instrumental in making personal computers the most vital tool of the modern age. Few dispute his business savvy, his perseverance, or his technical expertise, yet critics say he is ruthless in his dealings with competitors and driven more by his desire to maintain Microsoft's dominance in the computer industry than by an interest in furthering technology.

In these books, young readers will encounter inspiring stories about real people who achieved success despite enormous obstacles. Oprah Winfrey—one of the most powerful, most watched, and wealthiest women in television history—spent the first six years of her life in the care of her grandparents while her unwed mother sought work and a better life elsewhere. Her adolescence was colored by pregnancy at age fourteen, rape, and sexual abuse.

Each author documents and supports his or her work with an array of primary and secondary source quotations taken from diaries, letters, speeches, and interviews. All quotes are footnoted to show readers exactly how and where biographers derive their information and provide guidance for further research. The quotations enliven the text by giving readers eyewitness views of the life and accomplishments of each person covered in the People in the News series.

In addition, each book in the series includes photographs, annotated bibliographies, timelines, and comprehensive indexes. For both the casual reader and the student researcher, the People in the News series offers insight into the lives of today's newsmakers—people who shape the way we live, work, and play in the modern age.

The Stumble Seen Around the World

I t was Sunday, February 24, 2013—the evening of the annual Academy Awards ceremony in Hollywood, California. Typical of the Academy Awards, the program was running quite late; however, the excitement was electric because of the upcoming

Jennifer Lawrence slips on her way up to the stage to accept her Academy Award for Best Performance by an Actress in a Leading Role in 2013.

announcement of the Oscar for the category of Best Performance by an Actress in a Leading Role ("Best Actress," for short). Jean Dujardin, who had won the Best Actor award the previous year for *The Artist*, read the names of the nominees for Best Actress: Naomi Watts, Jessica Chastain, Emmanuelle Riva, Quvenzhané Wallis, and Jennifer Lawrence—Lawrence for her role in *Silver Linings Playbook*.

As Dujardin opened the envelope containing the winner's name, there was a hush in the audience. He read it, smiled, and announced, "And the Oscar goes to . . . Jennifer Lawrence!"[1] The cameras captured Jennifer's emotional, disbelieving, and somewhat tearful reaction, and the music began playing as she walked to the stage to claim her award. And then came the stumble. As she began walking up the steps leading to the stage, her foot caught on the bottom of her long gown, and she fell. Immediately, actor Hugh Jackman—who was sitting in the front row—jumped to his feet and ran to help her up. However, by the time he got to her side, Jennifer had righted herself and moved to the podium, flustered and clearly embarrassed.

A Standing Ovation

Meanwhile the audience had risen to its feet to applaud her win.

"You guys are just standing up because you feel bad that I fell," she joked. "That's really embarrassing."[2] She went on with her acceptance speech, thanking her costars and her family for their part in her success. But now the story was no longer that Jennifer Lawrence had become the youngest actress in history to be twice nominated for a Best Actress Oscar (and now had also become a winner); instead, her stumble coming to the stage would dominate the headlines.

Afterwards, in a backstage press conference, Jennifer was barraged with questions about her stumble. After one reporter asked what happened—and whether she had fallen on purpose—Jennifer smiled in confused disbelief at the question. "On purpose?" she laughed. "Absolutely! . . . What do you mean what happened? Look at my dress! I tried to walk up the stairs in this dress, that's what happened. Yeah, I think I just stepped on the fabric and . . . they [had] waxed the stairs."[3]

Asked what was going through her mind when she fell, she was honest: "A bad word that I can't say,"[4] she admitted, as the press laughed. Another reporter, noting that she had just won her first Oscar at the young age of twenty-two, asked whether Jennifer was worried about her career peaking too soon. Her smile faded, as she considered the question. "Well," she said, looking stricken, "*now* I am!"[5]

An Amazing Talent

Jennifer Lawrence is one of the most talked-about celebrities in Hollywood. As of 2014, she had been nominated for three Academy Awards, winning Best Actress for her performance in *Silver Linings Playbook*. She is in demand for appearances on television talk shows because of her frankness and good humor, and she has the rare blend of beauty, talent, and candor. "Whether lighting up an indie [independent film] or fronting a blockbuster franchise," notes *Vogue* magazine, "Jennifer Lawrence is the most electric talent to hit Hollywood in a generation."[6]

Lawrence's meteoric rise to stardom is itself like something from a Hollywood film. As a fourteen-year-old, she was able to persuade her parents to let her go to New York and give acting a try. With no formal acting training, and certainly not coming from a family of actors, the odds of her success were incredibly slim. Even so, she had unwavering confidence in herself and would not be denied. As she later recalled, even when her friends were skeptical about her chances of becoming a star, she never stopped believing. "When I first got to New York, my feet hit the sidewalk and you'd have thought I was born and raised there. I took over that town. None of my friends took me seriously. I came home and announced, 'I'm going to move to New York,' and they were, like, 'OK.' Then when I did, they kept waiting for me to fail and come back. But I knew I wouldn't. I was, like, 'I'll show you.'"[7]

Almost a decade later, Jennifer Lawrence has achieved more than many actors have in a lifetime of work. She has accomplished with grace (most of the time) and a sense of humor the goals she set for herself. She has endeared herself to fans with not only her uncanny acting talents but also her ability to maintain a sense of humility—something rare in Hollywood.

Asked whether she finds it difficult to keep her perspective amid such acclaim, she replies:

> Not to sound rude, but [acting] is stupid. Everybody's like, "How can you remain with a level head?" And I'm, like, why would I ever get cocky? I'm not saving anybody's life. There are doctors who save lives and firemen who run into burning buildings. I'm making movies.[8]

Little wonder that fans can hardly wait to see what project she will take on next.

Chapter 1

Growing Up Nitro

Jennifer Shrader Lawrence was born on August 15, 1990, in a suburb of Louisville, Kentucky, called Indian Hills. Her father, Gary, owned a concrete contracting company called Lawrence and Associates, and her mother, Karen, ran a day camp for children called Camp Hi-Ho. Jennifer is the youngest of three children; she has two older brothers, Ben and Blaine. The news of Karen's third pregnancy had been a surprise. "We thought we were finished having kids," Karen admits. "We [had gotten] rid of the baby bed and everything."[9]

Growing Up Tough

While her parents were excited about having a daughter, Karen was adamant that her little girl would not become a pampered diva. Although she was the baby of the family, little Jennifer was not exempt from her brothers' teasing and roughhousing. "I didn't mind if she was girlie, as long as she was tough,"[10] Karen says.

The Lawrence family lived on a horse farm in Indian Hills, and Jennifer loved the open space, where she could ride and play. Evidently, being tough was not a problem. As early as preschool, her parents were getting notes from Jennifer's teacher saying that she was not allowed to play with the other girls because she was too rough. "She didn't mean to hurt them," Karen insists. "They were just making cookies, and she wanted to

Jennifer Lawrence's childhood home is in the Louisville, Kentucky, suburb of Indian Hills. Having a good sense of humor is highly valued in Lawrence's family, which includes two older brothers.

play ball."[11] Her energetic personality earned her the nickname Nitro.

But Jennifer says she learned toughness at home from her brothers, who treated her like one of the boys. "Being the youngest and the only girl, I think everyone was so worried about me being a brat that they went in the exact opposite direction. I'd slap my brother on the arm and he'd throw me down the stairs. I was always like, 'Can we talk about excessive force, please?'"[12]

A Crucial Sense of Humor

She recalls how central comedy was to her family. To survive in the Lawrence family, she says, you had to have a sense of humor. "My mom is big funny. She is loud funny," Jennifer says. "And my dad is the opposite—the funniest person you will ever meet, but he never raises his voice. He's just really quick. Very subtle."[13]

In fact, sometimes her father's humor is so subtle that an outsider may not understand he is joking. In a 2011 interview for *Elle* magazine, Jennifer gives an example of her father's dry wit. It occurred just before she was leaving on her first date with Nicholas Hoult, the British actor who is one of her costars in the *X-Men* movies:

> When Nick and I went on our first date, my parents were visiting, in London, and my dad goes, "Jen, have you told him I don't mind going back to prison?" Nick didn't bring it up until later, in the cab. He's like, "So . . . when was your dad in prison?" The meaner my family is, the more you're in. When my family's nice and stiff, that's when you're in trouble.[14]

At Comic-Con 2013 in San Diego, California, Peter Dinklage (left), Jennifer Lawrence, and Nicholas Hoult play a joke with their name signs. Hoult dated Lawrence and was a target of her family's dry wit.

Her two brothers, she says, are hysterically funny. They have always been able to make her laugh—even when she is in a terrible mood. Much of their humor involves making fun of her anytime she begins to take herself too seriously. She remembers one occasion when the three of them were standing in line at a grocery store in Louisville and noticed that her picture was on the cover of several magazines on display near the counter. She felt embarrassed, realizing that people might be put off by her overexposure. "I was like, God, I'm going to be one of those people everybody hates, because it's like, 'Hey, here I am!,' like, all the time, and it's just, like, 'Get out of my face.' And [my brothers] were, like, 'No, everybody hates you because you're ugly.'"[15]

Early Talent

Her interest in acting and entertaining started when Jennifer was a little girl. She loved reading and was riveted by the stories her mother read to her. She also had an amazing memory for stories as a child, and her family has the home video to prove it. When Jennifer was only three years old, her grandfather was telling stories, which she already had memorized. On the video, the toddler corrects her grandfather each time he forgets to mention what she considers an important detail of the story.

Jennifer also loved to watch the movies her brothers were watching—especially comedies like *Ace Ventura: Pet Detective* and *Dumb and Dumber*. Her family says that by the time she was a kindergartner, she could quote funny lines from Adam Sandler's popular movie *Billy Madison*.

Her parents say that she watched television as a little girl, but in a different way than their sons did. At first they assumed that when she was glued to the television, she was simply enjoying herself. In hindsight, however, they now realize that she was figuring things out. Rather than just watching the shows, her mother recalls, she was studying them, watching how the comedians delivered their lines.

One of her favorite routines was that of comedians Will Ferrell and Cheri Oteri, who performed a popular skit about two cheerleaders named Craig and Ariana on *Saturday Night Live*.

Jennifer Lawrence is a fan of Will Ferrell and Cheri Oteri's cheerleader characters (pictured) from Saturday Night Live, and she amused friends and family performing their TV skits.

Not good enough to make the school cheerleading squad for football and basketball, Craig and Ariana show up in uniform to cheer at other events, such as chess tournaments. Yelling and cheering for their school chess champ (which is funny because chess tournaments are held in silence), the cheerleaders scream taunts like, "K-I-N-G, you can't take my king from me—you're ugly! You're ugly!"[16] Jennifer, who was not at all shy, enjoyed performing the cheerleading routines to the amusement of her family and friends.

Being Different

For a little girl as bright, outgoing, and energetic as Jennifer, one might think that heading off to school would have been a fabulous experience—but it was not. "I was hyperactive, curious about everything," she recalls. "When my mother told me about my childhood, she always told me there was like a light in me, a spark that inspired me constantly. When I entered the school, the light went out."[17]

She had no trouble making friends, but she was frequently very anxious. "I was a weirdo," she says. "I wasn't picked on or anything. And I wasn't smarter than the other kids. . . . I've always just had this weird anxiety. I hated recess. I didn't like field trips. Parties really stressed me out. And I had a very different sense of humor."[18]

She told *Vogue* reporter Jonathan Van Meter that as a little girl, she often targeted her family with her humor. At age ten, she sometimes rang the doorbell of her home and pretended to be someone else when a family member answered. "Hi," she would say, "my name is Susan. My car broke down up the street, and I'm wondering if I could come in and use your phone."[19]

Another example of her offbeat humor was the way she decided to deal with a terrible haircut she received when she was in middle school. Jennifer had just returned to school after a family vacation—a cruise. She had gotten a haircut while on the cruise, and the result, she remembers, was hideous. But instead of keeping a low profile, she decided to call attention to herself and her terrible haircut. "I had, like, this blonde curly [Afro], and I walked into the gym the first day back in seventh grade and everyone was staring at me, and for some reason I thought, I know what I need to do! And I just started sprinting from one end of the gym to the other, and I thought it was hilarious. But nobody else at that age really did. It was genuinely weird."[20]

Dealing with Mean People

Another somewhat painful school memory also involved middle school. A girl named Meredith, who did not like Jennifer, asked her for a favor: Would Jennifer mind handing out a stack of invitations to Meredith's birthday party? Cruelly, Meredith had not included an invitation for Jennifer. "Who does that?" Jennifer asks, still amazed almost ten years later. "You're just outing yourself as mean."[21]

She dealt with it with confidence and her devil-may-care attitude rather than feeling humiliated. "I started whistling," Jennifer remembers, "and I walked over to the trash can and I dumped them in. Then when I had a birthday party, I invited her. I won."[22]

She had friends but continued to suffer from anxiety. She took medication for this condition, and, finally, her parents took her to a therapist, but neither seemed to help. She continued to work hard in school; she joined the cheerleading squad. She was even voted "Most Talkative" in seventh grade. But there was something missing, her mother says, looking back on those days. "She never fit in anywhere."[23]

Early Interest in Acting

Interestingly, one of the activities Jennifer enjoyed the most was playing a role, just as she had when she was a little girl acting out *Saturday Night Live* comedy skits. Taking on a different person's mannerisms, a different way of speaking, and even a new way of walking was exciting for her.

Her first time onstage was at Christ Methodist Church in Louisville, in a play about the biblical prophet Jonah. Nine-year-old Jennifer had only a small part—playing one of the prostitutes from the ancient city of Nineveh—but she decided to make the most of it. "The other girls just stood there with lipstick on," her mother recalls, "but she came in swinging her booty and strutting her stuff. Our friends said, 'We don't know if we should congratulate you or not, because your kid's a great prostitute.'"[24]

That would not have surprised Christopher Noah, who taught ancient history when Jennifer was in middle school. Noah recalls that Jennifer stood out because she liked to dramatize the mythology stories they studied. "If we were doing something about Cupid and Psyche," he says, "Jen would take the role of Psyche and change her voice and mannerisms."[25]

Spending Time at the Walden Theatre

When she was in eighth grade, she began taking acting classes at Louisville's Walden Theatre, a respected organization for young people to explore acting as a way of expressing themselves. Jennifer got the role of Desdemona in Shakespeare's *Othello* and thoroughly enjoyed the experience.

Charlie Sexton, the artistic director at Walden, recalls how remarkable her talent was for such a young girl. And while he was not surprised that she achieved success in acting, he was stunned at how fast it happened, commenting:

> She was inquisitive, eager, and attentive in class. I remember she did a scene from *Othello*, and she picked it up very quickly. She learned very quickly. I knew she was going to go places. I didn't realise it would be so quick, but [Jennifer] said, "I'm going to do this." We didn't get a lot of eighth graders saying, "I'm going to New York." I got a sense that she was way more determined than most of the kids her age. . . . I've seen her movies. My sense was that she didn't need a lot of directing, she just picked up stuff straight away.[26]

Looking back on that time, however, her mother admits that the family did not realize what a good actor Jennifer was. Though her family was happy and supportive of her experiences at Walden and in the plays at church, they did not understand

Getting a Second Opinion

Not surprisingly, Jennifer's parents were quite reluctant to allow their teenaged daughter to start a show business career. And even though Charlie Sexton of the Walden Theatre was impressed by her talent and was optimistic about her chances of success, Karen and Gary Lawrence decided to seek another opinion. They approached Flo Salant Greenberg, a highly respected acting coach and trainer. Greenberg has taught several highly successful actors, including Kirsten Dunst, Katherine Heigl, and Matt LeBlanc, who played Joey Tribbiani on the popular television show *Friends*.

After watching Jennifer work, Greenberg was clearly impressed, saying, "Jennifer has incredible instincts. As an acting coach, you look for people who have excellent emotional instincts and Jen is one of those rare people who work from [their] own natural instincts. Consequently, when she came to me, she was brilliantly talented." She added, "She's very rare; you [seldom] come across young people with that [talent]. . . . She was so loaded with good, genuine talent that her own instincts came through beautifully. I'm hoping that she lets that alone and just works on her own, which I assume she's doing. She's doing a brilliant job."

Greenberg told Jennifer's parents that their daughter had a bright future in acting and described Lawrence as "lovely," "versatile," and "sensitive." . . . "She was wonderful. I think that she's going to do extremely well."

Quoted in Iona Kirby and Hugo Daniel. "Fresh-Faced *Hunger Games* Star Jennifer Lawrence Pictured Before She Was Famous." *Daily Mail*.com, March 27, 2012. www.dailymail .co.uk/tvshowbiz/article-2121264/Fresh-faced-Jennifer-Lawrence-pictured-famous --acting-coaches-praise-natural-talent.html.

how good she was. "In our family, everything was about sports," Karen Lawrence says. "If she could've thrown a baseball, we would have been able to tell that she could pitch. We just didn't recognize her talent."[27]

A Vacation in New York

That recognition came in the spring of 2004. More than anything else, Jennifer wanted to start her acting career right away. She had no intention of waiting until she was older, and it was clear that the opportunities in Kentucky were limited. She had

Siblings Ben, Jennifer, and Blaine Lawrence (left to right) attend the 2013 Film Independent Spirit Awards in Santa Monica, California. At age fourteen, Jennifer persuaded her parents to let her stay with Blaine for a summer in New York City to continue auditioning.

Jennifer Lawrence (center) and her parents, Gary and Karen, attend a party for one her films in 2012.

called a talent agency in New York and had set up an interview. The only hurdle was getting her parents to agree.

When she first asked her parents to let her go to New York for the interview, they were reluctant. Finally, however, her mother agreed to go with her during Jennifer's middle school's spring break. "I really thought, let's just get this over with and go to spring break, and you'll hear 'Don't let the door hit you on the way out' so many times,'" admits Karen Lawrence. "I would have never taken her if I thought something actually would have happened, so the joke was on me."[28]

"The Exact Opposite of Stage Parents"

Jennifer laughs when asked by reporters about whether her parents might have pushed her to be an actress. She gives the example of when she and her mother visited the talent agency. The agency asked her to do what is called a "cold reading"—a reading from a script that she had never seen before, to see what kind of acting ability she possessed.

The agency representatives were highly impressed with her reading. In fact, they told Jennifer that it was the best cold read they had ever had from a fourteen-year-old. But her mother was not convinced the agency was being truthful. She worried that perhaps the staff was raising her hopes unfairly. Most of all, she did not want them to take advantage of her daughter.

"My mom told me they were lying," Jennifer remembers. "My parents were the exact opposite of stage parents. They did everything in their power to keep it from happening. But it was going to happen no matter what. I was, like, 'Thanks for raising me, but I'm going to take it from here.'"[29]

After leaving the agency that afternoon, Jennifer and her mother stopped to watch an H&M clothing commercial being filmed in Union Square in Manhattan. As they stopped to watch the dancers, a photographer with the company filming the commercial approached Jennifer and asked whether she would allow him to take her picture. Her mother reluctantly agreed, and after taking several photographs, he wrote down Jennifer's contact information.

The following day, Jennifer got a telephone call from the photographer's agency, inviting her to his studio to audition for a Reese's Peanut Butter Puff cereal commercial. And while she did not get that job, the agency was optimistic about her future. They wanted to work with Jennifer and urged her to spend the rest of the summer in New York. They could see that she was good enough to get work in other commercials.

A Summer in New York

Jennifer was eager to remain in the city to continue auditioning, but Gary and Karen Lawrence were not sold on the idea. Karen could not remain in New York during the summer months, because she ran the summer camp, and her father worked full-time. And there was no way that they would allow their daughter to stay in New York without adult supervision. Finally, her parents agreed to let her stay for six weeks, and her nineteen-year-old brother, Blaine, would stay with her.

During that time, Jennifer was invited to more and more auditions, and her confidence grew. Finally, she was chosen to do a Verizon commercial and admits that she was thrilled to meet the "Can you hear me now?" man. She also got a very small part in the television show *Monk*; however, she was unrecognizable because she played a team mascot and wore a cougar suit while dancing around the bleachers leading cheers. She was also in a Burger King commercial and did a televised promotional piece for the MTV series *My Sweet Sixteen*.

Not every audition was successful, however. She laughs when remembering how the agency sent her to a Los Angeles photo shoot for the clothing company Abercrombie & Fitch. Jennifer was one of several kids who were playing on a beach. The photographer had tossed them a football and instructed them to have fun playing. But while Jennifer thought she had done well, it turned out that none of the photos in which she appeared were used. Out of curiosity, her father called and asked the agency why. The agency representative sent over the negatives to show him, laughs Jennifer, recalling that in the photos "all the other girls are looking cute, modeling while playing football. And my face is bright red, my nostrils are flared, and I'm in mid-leap, about to tackle this girl, like 'Rahhrrr!' I'm not even looking at the camera. The other girls were like, 'Get her away from me!'"[30]

A Serious Decision

As the end of summer approached, Jennifer wanted to stay in New York. She was getting more and more opportunities to work; however her parents were not in favor of it. They strongly believed that her education had to come first and were not convinced that an acting career was the right thing for Jennifer, who had just turned fifteen in August. But Blaine and Ben came to Jennifer's defense. They reminded their parents that they had traveled all over the country for their baseball and football

A Loyal Friend from Junior High

Twenty-three-year-old Andy Strunk, who has Down syndrome, is an old friend of Jennifer's from Louisville. The two have been good friends since they met at church and later as students at Kammerer Middle School. "She has always had a soft heart for him," Andy's mother, Pollyana, says. "She always looked out for him. Middle school is a tough place to be, especially for a kid with special needs."

Jennifer was voted "Most Talkative" in seventh grade, and she began her own campaign to elect Andy to be chosen as "Mr. Kammerer"—an honor that lets a student be king for the day. "She nominated him, and he won," says Pollyana. "She would talk to her friends and tell them to vote for him. She is very charismatic. It's just her natural person coming out."

Today, with Jennifer a megastar in Hollywood, Andy says she is the same friendly girl she has always been. She sends Andy signed pictures and posters and other memorabilia that he keeps on his wall. To bring his friend good luck on awards nights, Andy dresses up in a tuxedo to watch the ceremony on television. And whenever Jennifer is back in Louisville, she always stops over to spend time with Andy, who considers her one of his very best friends.

Quoted in Simone Weichselbaum. "Family and Friends Say Oscar Winner Jennifer Lawrence Is Still a Down-Home Kentucky Girl." *New York Daily News*, March 3, 2013. www .nydailynews.com/entertainment/gossip/oscar-winner-jennifer-lawrence-down-home -ky-girl-article-1.1277980.

games. "This is her baseball diamond," they said. "You gotta let her play."[31]

Her parents relented, but to get a realistic idea of their daughter's likelihood of succeeding at acting, they consulted Flo Greenberg, a famed acting coach. Greenberg had worked with such well-known actors as Kirsten Dunst and Matt LeBlanc (who played Joey Tribbiani on the popular television series *Friends*).

After assessing Jennifer's abilities, Greenberg was impressed. "I was eager for her to pursue her acting career immediately," she recalls. "I don't say that about many people. Sometimes, you need to know when to keep your hands off and let somebody's natural technique blossom."[32]

But there was still one element that worried her parents: school. They were concerned that she would miss out on her education, and they were adamant that she needed to at least finish high school—no matter how talented she was. They finally came to an agreement: Jennifer could take classes online to complete the courses that she would be missing while pursuing her acting career. Her mother and father would take turns living in the New York apartment with her, to make sure she did her schoolwork. As it turned out, she finished her high school work in two years with a 3.9 grade-point average, which made her parents very proud.

Now What?

One thing was certain: Even though her parents had their doubts about the wisdom of their teenager's career choice, she was clearly happier than she had ever been. When she was in junior high, she was anxious and unsure of herself, but in front of a camera or onstage Jennifer was confident and strong. "We're paying for therapy and all this medication," said Karen when she called her husband from one of Jennifer's shoots in New York, "but she doesn't need it when she's here. She's *happy*."[33]

As the months went by, Jennifer was getting more and more opportunities for auditions. She had a small role in an episode of the TV drama *Cold Case* and appeared in two episodes of *Medium*. It became clear that, at least for the moment, Jennifer was having enough success for them to invest in a second home-away-from-home for when Jennifer was working in California. They bought a condo in Santa Monica, and Karen would make the trip from Kentucky to California to stay with Jennifer whenever she was filming there.

It was certainly not an ideal situation for the family. When her parents had doubts about whether they should let Jennifer continue, they reminded themselves how important it was to their daughter. Jennifer was aware of their sacrifice. She knew how stressful it was for her parents to be apart for weeks at a time and how expensive it was to maintain two extra homes, including an apartment in New York. "My parents saw me so truly happy that they sacrificed everything for my happiness," she says. "Without my family, I would be nothing."[34]

But no one—except, perhaps, Jennifer—could have predicted just how successful she would be.

Chapter 2

Early Successes

As she became more and more comfortable with auditions for acting roles and commercials in 2005 and 2006, Lawrence was becoming more successful at finding work. She continued to do commercials and won small parts on television shows. In 2007, she was excited to win a part on a new television sitcom written by and starring comedian Bill Engvall.

The Bill Engvall Show

The Bill Engvall Show was about a fictional family in Denver, Colorado, with comedian Engvall playing the part of a family therapist. Though he was successful at his job, Engvall's own family was giving him fits—especially his eldest, Lauren, played by Lawrence. Lauren's character was a typical teenager, testing the limits and rules of parents and teachers and dealing with dating and peer pressure—as well as her two brothers.

The show ran for three seasons (thirty episodes) before being canceled in September 2009. And while reviews of the show were mixed, Lawrence insisted that it was a wonderful experience. She particularly enjoyed the camaraderie she felt with the cast and crew. "*The Bill Engvall Show*, I'm so grateful for it," she told reporters later. "I had so much fun on that show, and we all became like family."[35]

Engvall also enjoyed the experience and remembers being very impressed by Lawrence's work. Afterward, he predicted

Jennifer Lawrence and Graham Patrick Martin act in a scene for **The Bill Engvall Show,** *Lawrence's first major acting role.*

that big things were in store for the young actress. "Of my favorite scenes that I did on that show, one of them was with Jennifer," he remembers. "I go back and watch it every once in a while. We had a scene where she was mad at me and I had to go in and apologize to her. We had that nice dad–daughter moment. I remember [thinking], 'This girl's good.' She's got it; she's got what it takes. I think she'll be holding that [award] statuette before she's done."[36]

Lawrence was glad to have consistent work during that time. In addition to providing her with a steady paycheck, she also had breaks between seasons—time that she used to audition for other parts. One of these auditions was for the role of Bella Swan in the popular movie *Twilight*. And while Lawrence did not get the part, she did find a niche in smaller independent films during this time. Interestingly, it would be not in a blockbuster movie like *Twilight*, but rather, her work in a handful of small independent films that would kick-start Lawrence's meteoric rise to fame.

The Poker House

Independent films (known as "indies") are films that have far smaller budgets than big Hollywood blockbusters—just a fraction of what a studio like Paramount, Time-Warner, or 20th Century Fox spends making a movie. Most of the time—although not always—the actors in an indie are not well known, and the style of the film tends to be more artistic than big-studio movies. During her break between seasons of *The Bill Engvall Show*, Lawrence auditioned for an indie called *The Poker House*, written and directed by actress Lori Petty, who had starred with Tom Hanks, Geena Davis, Madonna, and Rosie O'Donnell in the popular 1992 movie *A League of Their Own*.

Released in 2008 with a budget of only $1.5 million, *The Poker House* shows a single day in the life of a family of a mother and three sisters in Iowa in 1976. They live in what is known as the Poker House, a house of prostitution where criminals and pimps also gather to play poker. The house is run by the girls' mother, Sarah, played by Selma Blair. Having fled her marriage to a minister who used to beat her and their daughters, Sarah is now a drug and alcohol addict, as well as a prostitute, and is unable to adequately care for her daughters.

The role for which Lawrence was being considered (and was eventually cast) was that of the eldest sister, fourteen-year-old Agnes, who is essentially raising her two younger sisters, twelve-year-old Bee and eight-year-old Cammie. Agnes loves to read and play basketball on her high school's team. But the film's most shocking moment is when Agnes is brutally raped by her mother's pimp, played by David Alan Grier. Even after the rape, Agnes is somehow able to summon the strength to be there for her younger sisters. At the end of the film, it is revealed that the movie was actually a true story of Lori Petty's life before she went to Hollywood and became a successful actor, screenwriter, and director.

Lori Petty co-wrote and directed the film The Poker House. *The character played by Jennifer Lawrence in the film is based on Petty herself.*

"The Camera Loves Her"

Looking back on that time, Lawrence admits that it was not the script's merits that made her choose to audition for *The Poker House*. In fact, she did not know how good the film was until years later, as she tells an interviewer:

> I was young. I hadn't done anything else and so everything that I read I wanted to do. But now that I'm older and actually have a point of view and I can see what an amazing, brilliant script it is and how it grabs you and it has teeth and it's real and it's ugly and all the things that aren't usually appealing really appeal to me. . . . It was a movie. I auditioned for it. I got it, and then I just started acting. Now I can really look back on it and appreciate it.[37]

Lawrence was unsure about the movie at the time, but she was not the only one. Director Petty had doubts about Lawrence's playing the role of Agnes—not only because of her inexperience but because she was far taller than veteran actor Blair, who had already been cast as the mother. Petty later recalled how casting director Mary Vernieu had sent over tapes of several girls that could play the role.

"Mary sends me these tapes of these girls and goes, 'This girl Jennifer Lawrence is a *star*. You have to watch this tape.' But it said [Lawrence] was 5'9" on her resume, and I said, 'I can't fit them both in the frame! How am I supposed to have the mom be 5' and the daughter be 5'9"?' But [Mary] said, 'Just watch the tape.'"[38]

Petty agreed to look at the tape and was astonished at Lawrence's talent. She said later that it was much like a moment many years earlier when she and director Penny Marshall were working on *A League of Their Own* and were approached by Robert De Niro, who was working on a film called *This Boy's Life* with a young, unknown actor named Leonardo DiCaprio in the same building where Petty and Marshall were working.

> So De Niro comes in and goes, "You've got to see this kid."
> So we went into the room and saw some unedited scenes

Learning Who Is the Boss

As Lawrence's acting experience grew, from television roles to movies like *The Burning Plain* and *The Poker House*, she gradually learned about the relationship between an actor and the director, as she explains to reporter Brad Balfour of the *Huffington Post*.

> I view the director as my boss. I'm the pawn on the chess board. And though I'm not going to say anything stupid, there have been times that I've showed up and said, "I can't say that"—but after it goes through nine levels in my head of "Is this okay to say?"
>
> I don't say something to the director easily, because they are my boss. I think that the biggest problem—if I can speak openly with recorders around me, which is about to be a mistake—I think the biggest reason that actors are complete a-holes as soon as they become famous is because they forget that this is a job. They think it's about them, and it's not.
>
> We're making a film, and I never feel like I'm above anyone. . . . We are all doing the same thing, making a movie, except my face is going in front of the camera, and that's the only difference. You have to go behind the monitor and make sure I'm doing this right, let's come up with something to say, and then I'm going to say it in front of the camera, because that's my job, not because I'm awesome.

Quoted in Brad Balfour. "Best Actress Nominee Jennifer Lawrence Heats Up Winter's Bone." *Huffington Post*, February 25, 2011. www.huffingtonpost.com/brad-balfour/best-actress-jennifer-lawrence_b_828059.html.

with DiCaprio and both went, "There's another movie star." That's what happened with Jennifer.[39]

Petty says that she could tell right away that the sixteen-year-old Lawrence was going to be famous someday, the same way she knew with DiCaprio when she first saw him work. "She's amazing and the camera loves her, and that's why I cast her,"[40] she recalled later in an interview with the *Daily Beast* website.

Even with its limited budget, *The Poker House* garnered a great deal of attention. It premiered at the prestigious Los Angeles Film Festival and received great reviews—and much of that attention was focused on the young actress playing Agnes. For her work in the film, Lawrence received the Outstanding Performance Award at the festival.

Lessons Along the Way

Besides being proud of winning an award and becoming noticed by Hollywood producers and directors, Lawrence had learned important lessons by doing *The Poker House*, such as how valuable it was to work with talented actors, such as Blair.

Critics talk about certain actors as being "generous" or "giving" because they are especially supportive in scenes they do with other actors. That attitude is helpful to all of the other actors in the scene but is especially valuable to younger, less experienced actors like Lawrence then was. Lawrence comments:

> Selma is, I guess, a great actress. You can see that just by watching her, but she's such a giving actress, too. She [was] always giving me her eyes and was always listening and reacting to everything [my character was] saying, even when she's not on camera. The emotional scenes, that's all a part of acting. So I didn't get scared of any of it. She makes it a lot easier. When you work with an actress of that caliber, it just brings you up as well.[41]

Lawrence learned a great deal from Lori Petty's script, too—and what made it even more interesting was that *The Poker House* was a true story. In an interview with the movie-news website Collider, Lawrence recalls that it was not until they were well into the filming that she realized that the movie was autobiographical. Lawrence's role as Agnes was based on Petty's own childhood. "Nobody told me that I was playing Lori. I'd heard that it said 'based on a true story' in the script. I guess I didn't read the first page," Lawrence confesses. It dawned on her bit by bit, as she recounts:

Jennifer Lawrence, Lori Petty, and Selma Blair attend the screening of The Poker House *during the 2008 Los Angeles Film Festival.*

Little things would happen that I would kind of notice. Like [Lori] was really good at basketball [as Agnes was], and she would show me how to do certain things. Then the character in the movie has a huge book of e.e. cummings poems and has them all memorized, knows all of them. The set director brought that book on set and Lori was like, "Oh my gosh!" She goes straight to a page and [recites] every poem off the top of her head. I started to wonder, but I didn't want to ask anybody.[42]

Unpleasant Emotions

There was one aspect of doing the film that was not as pleasant. The story told in *The Poker House* was quite dark, and even though there is an inner strength within Agnes's character that helps her keep the family together, the film explores many powerful emotions—some of them very upsetting. For the sixteen-year-old Lawrence, some of those emotions would linger after the day's filming was finished. She said later that acting in the film was a little like taking part in a séance.

> It completely takes over you, and when it's gone, you're exhausted and you get confused about who you are, [and even] what your favorite food is. I know that sounds really weird, but I grew up in such a happy family. I really had nothing to compare this to. [Working on the film every day] I had to go to that dark place, which is a horrible, dark place to go, and it's hard to get out of that.[43]

This was a new experience for her, and as she explained in one interview, it had such profound emotional effect on her that she sought help from a therapist—and she is glad she did. "Now, fortunately, I know how to leave the character when I leave work. In fact, it leaves me after [the director calls] cut."[44]

The Burning Plain

Soon after filming *The Poker House*, Lawrence was cast in another indie—this one a crime drama called *The Burning Plain*. Written and directed by Mexican screenwriter Guillermo Arriaga, the film tells the story of Gina (played by Kim Bassinger), who is a cancer survivor, wife, and mother of four children living in a border town in New Mexico. Gina is having an extramarital affair with Nick, a local man who is married. Though Gina and Nick think they are being discreet, Gina's teenage daughter Mariana—Lawrence's character—discovers that the two are meeting in a trailer in a secluded place.

Determined to stop them from continuing the affair, Mariana decides to set fire to the trailer so that the couple will not have a place to meet. She is horrified, however, when the fire ignites

---

Opposite page: Jennifer Lawrence acts in a scene from **The Burning Plain.** *She was extremely nervous auditioning for the part, as it was only her second film.*

the trailer's gas tank, causing the trailer to explode, instantly killing her mother and Nick. *The Burning Plain* jumps backward and forward in time, showing viewers the effects of the tragedy on various characters, including Mariana as an adult (played by Charlize Theron).

Lawrence found herself extremely nervous about auditioning for the *The Burning Plain*. "I was terrified," she admits:

> I had only done one other movie, and the director [Lori Petty] really liked me. But I thought, "I [have] never done it before and I don't know what I'm doing. Am I going to be able to do it again?" I didn't have any trust in myself—but when I began, it felt exactly like the first one did; I started to trust myself a little bit more.[45]

And just as she had learned from working with Petty and Blair in *The Poker House*, Lawrence found Theron another interesting role model to learn from. It seemed that each new project was an experience that Theron used to expand her acting ability.

Mixed Reviews

The Burning Plain received varied reviews from both movie critics and audiences. Gary Goldstein of the *Los Angeles Times* was very positive, praising Lawrence's performance. London columnist Johanna Schneller singled out Lawrence's performance as one of the high points of the film, saying that "she grabbed my attention with her thousand-yard stare and her ability to convey a compelling inner life."[46]

The film was entered in the Sixty-Fifth Venice Film Festival in September 2008. The festival, an annual event held in Venice, Italy, celebrates the best in independent films from around the world. Lawrence and her family attended, and she later recalled how exciting it was to travel to Europe. "That was so fun because my family and I, at that time, had never been to Europe. And so we went two weeks beforehand; we traveled all around. By the time we got to Venice, we had spent so much time in the same clothes, crammed in a car eating Pringles. And then we got to Venice and all of a sudden we were in ball gowns."[47]

*The film **The Burning Plain** received mixed reviews, but Jennifer Lawrence's performance won the award for Best Young Actress at the 2008 Venice Film Festival in Italy.*

The Burning Plain did not win Best Film in any of the categories; however, Lawrence was speechless when it was announced that she had won the Marcello Mastroianni Award for Best Young Emerging Actress. It was her first time walking down the red carpet, and she beamed with excitement as she was presented with the award.

A New Audition

And while The Burning Plain did not attract large audiences, one important viewer was a director named Debra Granik. She was in the midst of casting a new movie, called Winter's Bone, which was based on a 2006 novel of the same title by Daniel Woodrell. The story revolves around a teenage girl named Ree Dolly who lives in the Ozarks of southwestern Missouri. Her father is a meth addict, and her mother is mentally ill and unable to care for herself. Ree is left to take care of her younger siblings, twelve-year-old Sonny and eight-year-old Ashlee, and teaches them to hunt and cook their own food.

The plot centers on Ree's search for her father, who disappeared after his arrest for making methamphetamine. He had put the family's house up for collateral on his bail, and the sheriff tells Ree that if he does not show up for his court date in one week, the family will be evicted from their home. The film follows Ree as she slogs through the bleak mountain backcountry, rife with poverty, drug use, long-standing grudges, and a clannish code of silence that prevents local people from assisting police or talking to outsiders about their neighbors.

"I'd Have Walk on Hot Coals to Get the Part"

Winter's Bone was familiar to Lawrence. Her mother had read the novel years before and commented that Ree would be a great character for Jennifer to play someday. "[She] said if they ever make it into a movie I would be perfect for it,"[48] Lawrence told a reporter from Filmmaker magazine.

Being Picky

Like other actors, Jennifer Lawrence has a staff that helps her navigate the auditions, interviews, appearances, and other responsibilities that are a big part of her job. In an interview with Marlowe Stern of *Manhattan Movie Magazine,* she explains the give-and-take that occurs between her and her staff when decisions need to be made.

I was pickiest when I picked my people. My publicity people know that if I'm being interviewed, if I'm on TV, if I'm in a magazine, I'm talking about work. I'm not talking about me and how I lost 10 pounds in two weeks. And then with movies, my agents know that I'm not going to do something that's stupid [or] if I don't love it. And they're OK with that. On the other hand, I do have a stylist, and she's a professional and I don't really argue with her. If she tells me to wear big pants, I'm going to wear them because she's a professional and not me. And if my publicity people tell me not to do this magazine, that's why I hired them—because I trust them. So, I won't do that magazine. If they had told me not to do *Winter's Bone,* I would have said, "Screw you. I'm doing it." But there are other movies where they'll say, "I don't think it's a good idea," and I won't do it.

Quoted in Marlowe Stern. "Jennifer Lawrence Is the Breakout Star of *Winter's Bone!*" *Manhattan Movie Magazine,* June 12, 2012. www.manhattanmoviemag.com/tag /marlow-stern/page/3.

But it was Lawrence's own reaction to Ree while reading the script that made her want to play the role. She loved the fact that the star of the movie was a young woman—especially a young woman of seventeen—and that she was not paired with a strong, capable man, as in so many other movie scripts. "I admired [Ree]," she recalls. "She has a strength that I could never

Jennifer Lawrence's mother read the novel Winter's Bone *and thought the part of Ree in the film adaptation would be perfect for her daughter.*

possess, and . . . you just find yourself fascinated with the life that she has and the attitude that she has toward it."[49]

Lawrence decided at once that she would use Ree's determination and perseverance to win the role. "I'd have walked on hot coals to get the part," she admits. "I thought it was the best female role I'd read—ever. I was so impressed by Ree's tenacity and that she didn't take no for an answer."[50]

When Granik announced open auditions in Los Angeles, New York, and Missouri (where the movie was being shot), hundreds showed up. Lawrence was determined to get the part. She auditioned in Los Angeles but was told that her looks were wrong for the film—she was simply too pretty for the part. But Lawrence would not be deterred. She said later that she was so eager to get the role of Ree that she became almost obsessed with it. Knowing that after the Los Angeles auditions, Granik and producer Anne Rosellini were heading to New York to oversee the auditions there, she followed them. She boarded a flight to New York, intent on proving to Granik and Rosellini that she was the best choice to play Ree.

The Audition That Changed Everything

After being eliminated in Los Angeles because of her looks, Lawrence was determined to downplay her good looks for her New York audition. She took the red-eye flight to New York, and when she arrived, she walked thirteen blocks to the audition, even though it was windy and sleeting. "[I] had to be as ugly as possible," she says. "I didn't wash my hair for a week, I had no makeup on. I looked beat up in there. I think I had icicles hanging from my eyebrows."[51] She made no attempt to comb her hair before her name was called to audition—and Granik and Rosellini were more impressed this time.

"She looked very physical and athletic, which we always imagined Ree would be," Rosellini recalls, "and she had a great voice—a sort of deep, earthy-tone quality, which we appreciated. We also knew she didn't sleep much (on the flight) and that may have brought an air of desperation or of haggardness to her that maybe a normal 18-year-old wouldn't have. Maybe we responded to that."[52] Granik agrees, adding that Lawrence's native Kentucky accent was also a plus. While hearing Lawrence audition in New York, Granik felt that "for the first time, . . . I was really hearing Ree."[53]

Elated that her tenacity had paid off, Lawrence was impatient to get to work on filming *Winter's Bone*. Although she knew she loved the character and the story, she had no idea that this film would springboard her into the public eye more than any other role she had played so far. Not only would she become known for her skill as an actress, she also would have an only-dreamed-about opportunity to walk the red carpet at the Academy Awards for her portrayal of Ree Dolly.

Chapter 3

Jennifer's Big Break

Before any filming took place on *Winter's Bone*, director Debra Granik talked with Lawrence about how she envisioned the film's production. Granik intended everything to be as authentic as possible, down to the last detail. There would be no movie sets built; instead, the entire film would be shot in real houses in the Ozark Mountains of Missouri. And Lawrence, who would be in every scene of the movie, would need to learn to do all the things that her character could do.

Working for "Authentic"

The film was scheduled to be shot over a period of twenty-six days. To make certain that Lawrence was comfortable in these surroundings, Granik insisted that Lawrence have a complete and sincere understanding of what existence was really like in the Ozarks—something movie actors rarely do. So, before filming began, Lawrence went to Missouri to live for a week with the Laysons, the mountain family on whose property they would be filming. She recalls:

> [Debra] wanted to make sure that I understood not only Ree but the life of the people there. . . . I spent enough time with the families and saw the way that they lived life [so] that I could play a girl growing up in that place. Ree was up to me, since I was the actor, but Debra wanted to make

sure I understood what it would be like for a girl my age to grow up in a home and in a family and in a place like the Ozarks.[54]

Also, the time she spent living with the Laysons resulted in an unexpected casting change. In Woodrell's novel, Ree had to care for two younger brothers, but while staying with the Laysons, Lawrence grew so close to their young daughter, Ashlee, that Granik made the decision to change the story a little bit and cast Ashlee as Ree's younger sister, instead of casting a younger brother.

Asked if she thought Ashlee enjoyed her acting debut, Lawrence stated, "I don't think she liked it. She had fun because we thought of it as make-believe, but she didn't like the camera, which I thought was awesome. I was like, you're going to be cool when you grow up. Because when I was a kid, I was like, where's the camera? So I'm always fascinated with little kids who are shy. I always think they're going to be way cooler than I could ever be."[55]

Becoming Ree Dolly

Some of Lawrence's preparation was very specific to her role as Ree Dolly. In addition to learning to chop wood, she needed to learn how to handle a shotgun, if her portrayal of Ree was to be realistic. While she was back in Kentucky before shooting began on the movie, her cousin taught her how to use a shotgun. "My cousin cleaned out a shotgun for me and let me carry it around the house," she told one interviewer, "because he said, 'Anybody who knows anything about guns is going to know in a second if someone has held a gun before.' I didn't want to be that person [who was unconvincing]. I wanted to be practiced."[56]

Lawrence also had concerns about her accent. It had impressed Granik and Rosellini during her audition, but while they were on location, it soon became clear to Lawrence that there was quite a difference between her natural Kentucky drawl and the way the mountain people in the Missouri Ozarks spoke. She comments:

Jennifer Lawrence wore the same outfit throughout the filming of **Winter's Bone.**

It worried me at first because Debra had recordings [of native Missourians speaking], and the people pronounced things a little bit differently. Every time I would try to speak, my Kentucky accent would come out. I just thought it was going to sound horrible. So I wrote Debra an email and said, "I don't know if I can do this," and she was, like, "Just speak in your Kentucky accent." She loved the way that I spoke. So that was a huge relief.[57]

Yellow Teeth, Old Clothes, and Homesickness

While in many Hollywood movies the lead—especially the female lead—would have lots of costume changes, *Winter's Bone* had virtually none. Lawrence wore the same jeans, flannel shirt, winter cap, and bulky jacket throughout the entire movie— and none of them were new. In fact, Lawrence later recalled, the wardrobe stylist had an ingenious method of making sure the clothing was authentic-looking. "She would trade [the local residents], like, new Carhartts [a brand of work clothes] for their used Carhartts—give them new clothes for their already-used clothes—and so I was wearing authentic, legitimate, been-worn-a-hundred-times jeans."[58]

In addition to banning a wardrobe of new clothes for the actors in *Winter's Bone*, Granik also put styled hair and white teeth on the "forbidden" list. Lawrence was not even allowed to wear lip balm the entire time of filming, because Granik wanted to have Ree's lips cracked from the cold winter wind. The worst part, Lawrence remembers, was what they did to her teeth and hair. "They yellowed my teeth every day, which sucked because I couldn't eat—which, you know, of course I did anyway—like every time I'd eat, I'd just get, like, a dirty look from the makeup artist. . . . They [also] messed up my hair—they put something in it, I'm not sure—I want to say they put, like, straight mud in my hair."[59]

While Lawrence was getting a drastic makeover on the outside, inside she was very homesick. Because she had turned eighteen, the filming for *Winter's Bone* was the first time she was not accompanied by one of her parents on the set, and she missed her family terribly. "Being away from home is my least favorite part of all of this," she admitted to reporter Jane Graham. "That really is the hardest part of my job."[60]

She finally decided to do something about it. Sobbing, she called her mother and asked her to come to Missouri. "She and my dad got in their car the next day," Lawrence remembers. "They're either that good of parents or I was that hysterical. No, I'm a baby; I am just not a very adult person when it comes to being alone."[61]

Making an Impression

The role of Ree Dolly was a difficult one and often physically challenging. John Hawkes, who costarred in the film as Ree's

Skinning a Squirrel

One of the most talked-about scenes of *Winter's Bone* was Ree Dolly's skinning a squirrel for the family's dinner. Because she hunted to keep her family alive, it was no surprise that a hunting scene would be part of the movie, but Lawrence was shocked to learn that there would be a scene in which she would be shown actually gutting and skinning a real squirrel.

While she was told before the filming what she was to do, she later admitted she found the entire experience very unpleasant because she finds squirrels cute. Even so, she believed that she could handle it—although it was far more difficult than she had anticipated. She describes her reaction once the scene was over:

> When they said, "Cut," I started shrieking and jumping up and down. Debra probably thought she miscast. I don't know. There was this weird mental place where I went to become Ree . . . . I honestly do think when you're working out and you're like, "I don't want to do it anymore," and then you're like, "I can do this, I'm a runner," then you can go another mile. I think I've gotten myself into that mentality of "I can chop this wood," and then I did. "I can cut open a squirrel and that's not going to gross me out until they call cut and then I'm going to shriek like a little girl."

Quoted in Brad Balfour. "Best Actress Nominee Jennifer Lawrence Heats Up *Winter's Bone*." Huffington Post, February 25, 2011. www.huffingtonpost.com/brad-balfour/best-actress-jennifer-lawrence_b_828059.html.

uncle Teardrop, was impressed by Lawrence's toughness in a scene in which he angrily grabs her by her hair. Granik shot the scene from different angles, so the hair-pulling went on for several takes. Hawkes said later that Lawrence had told him to "bring it" with each take—even though it would certainly hurt her.

John Hawkes, one of Jennifer Lawrence's costars in Winter's Bone, was impressed by Lawrence's ability to go in and out of character with ease between takes.

Hawkes was also impressed that she could distance herself from the role in between takes—something many actors cannot do. "Jennifer's the kind that can probably be in the middle of [telling] a joke, hear 'Action!' and cry, laugh, be angry or whatever she's got to do, and hear 'Cut!' and then say the punch line of the joke,"[62] he comments.

Granik was also highly complimentary about Lawrence's abilities as an actress. She said later that she was surprised by the ease with which the teenager made Ree her own and reacted differently to each of the characters she encountered in the film. "It's like taking an iconic American cowboy who doesn't say a whole lot, and what Jennifer did, instead of being a cardboard Western hero, was to make sure Ree didn't act the same with every character she meets. Jennifer's got a gift of being sensitive to the circumstances."[63]

Learning and Growing

By the end of filming, Lawrence realized that she had learned a great deal from the way Granik directed—and it has helped her as an actress. When they first began shooting *Winter's Bone*, Lawrence admits, she did not always understand what Granik was asking her to do:

> Debra has a brain that's not like ours. She has a mind that is on a whole other playing field. It took me awhile to get in sync with that, because for a while it was like reading instructions, like this is just too smart for me. If I could only understand what the instructions meant, I could get this radio going, but I just don't get it. Once you start understanding her, you start realizing she is a genius—her attention to detail, though, of course is so annoying at the time, because it's, like, "Do I really have to do that scene again? Do I really have to do it this way?" Then I watched it in the movie, and I thought, "What if Debra hadn't made me do that again?"[64]

Lawrence was also impressed with the director's insistence on learning from the local people. It was not only the scenery and clothing that had to be authentic, she says. "[Granik] dedicated everything to staying with this [Ozark] family and asking them, 'How do you do this? How do you do that?' She wouldn't put anything on camera without it being authentic."[65]

Besides acquiring respect for her costars and director, Lawrence was quick to defend the local mountain people, who are often negatively stereotyped. Asked by reporters about the abuse of women that is notable in the film, Lawrence argued that while there are cultural differences, the people of the Missouri Ozarks are not much different from other Americans:

> Women there have to ask to use their husband's truck, but women in [New York City] have husbands saying they're at the office late when they're really sleeping with their secretary. And the women stay. So many people feel sympathy for the women in this film, but I don't—they're perfectly fine. Their houses and cars aren't as nice, but they probably feel sorry for us because we don't have dinner with our families every night. It's just different. I don't think women are treated any worse, it's just more out in the open.[66]

Going to Sundance

Once the filming was finished, the next goal was to showcase *Winter's Bone*. Since, as a rule, indies do not have the budget for promotions that major studio movies do, they are often debuted in film festivals to give them publicity. Just as the producers of *The Burning Plain* entered the film in the Venice Film Festival, Granik and Rosellini submitted *Winter's Bone* to the Sundance Film Festival, held annually in Park City, Utah. Granik and her staff hoped that Sundance would be a launching pad for a wider audience for their film; however, only a handful of films each year are accepted into Sundance, so they waited nervously to learn whether or not *Winter's Bone* would be chosen.

They were thrilled when they found that Sundance had chosen it from among 3,724 submissions to compete with fifteen other films in the U.S. Drama category. Lawrence knew that just being accepted for inclusion at Sundance was a huge honor, and she remembers crying with joy when the cast and crew heard the news.

But her excitement soon turned into jubilation when *Winter's Bone* was announced as the winner of the Grand Jury Prize for

The cast of the film Winter's Bone *attend the Sundance Film Festival in 2010. The film went on to win the festival's Grand Jury Prize.*

a Dramatic Film. Having won that honor, the film drew a great deal of public attention when it was released in theaters. Later, Lawrence would recall how amazed she was that so many people had seen the film—even with its success at Sundance—because indies rarely attract the crowds that Hollywood movies do. Once, when someone stopped her on the street and complimented her on *Winter's Bone*, she was incredulous. She recalls, "I was like, 'You saw *Winter's Bone*?'"[67]

Raves and Awards

Besides drawing substantial numbers of moviegoers, *Winter's Bone* attracted a great deal of attention from movie critics after the Sundance Festival. A.O. Scott of the *New York Times* praised the film, noting that while its rural mountain setting is powerful, it is Lawrence's portrayal of Ree Dolly that stands out. According to Scott, "Its setting is finally subordinate to the main character, as memorable and vivid a heroine as you are likely to see on screen this season."[68]

Critic David Denby of the *New Yorker* was also highly complimentary, writing that *Winter's Bone* was a rare film that was both artistic and suspenseful. "[It] is what we've been waiting for: a work of art that grabs hold and won't let go," he writes. Denby also praised Lawrence's performance as a key part of the success of *Winter's Bone*, noting that "the movie would be unimaginable with anyone less charismatic playing Ree. . . . She's not just the most interesting teenager around, she's more believable as a heroic character than any of the men we've seen peacocking through movies recently."[69]

In addition to the Sundance Festival award, *Winter's Bone* and its cast began to receive other awards. In December 2010, Lawrence won the award for The Most Promising Performer from the Chicago Film Critics Association and the Best Actress award from Sweden's Stockholm Film Festival. She also won the Hollywood Film Festival Award for Best Breakthrough Performance. Making the latter experience even more memorable for Lawrence was that Academy Award–winning actress Jodie Foster introduced her and presented her with the award.

Oscar Buzz

But of all the accolades *Winter's Bone* was receiving, the most exciting was the attention coming from the Academy of Motion Picture Arts and Sciences, the organization that votes for the Academy Awards, or Oscars, as they are familiarly called.

Rather than being thrilled at the idea of being nominated for an Oscar, however, Lawrence was very uncomfortable with the

Jennifer Lawrence acts in a scene from **Winter's Bone.** *Her performance was praised by movie critics after the film was shown at a number of festivals around the world.*

subject. Her mother had e-mailed her a newspaper article one night about the possibility of Lawrence being nominated for an Oscar. Lawrence's reaction was to promptly shut her computer. The very idea terrified her. Asked by a reporter whether she had thought about where she might display the gold statue if she were to win one, Lawrence was nearly panic stricken. "I put my fingers in my ears and go la-la-la every time I hear that word," she said. "I have no idea how to talk about an Oscar at 20 years old. I can, like, make a dentist appointment, barely. I don't even know how to shop online!"[70]

On the morning of January 25, 2011, however, the nominees for Academy Awards were announced. *Winter's Bone* was nominated for Best Picture, along with big Hollywood hits such as *The King's Speech, The Social Network, Toy Story 3, The Black*

Critical Acclaim for
Winter's Bone

Besides drawing substantial numbers of moviegoers, *Winter's Bone* attracted a great deal of attention from movie critics after the Sundance Festival. Critic A.O. Scott of the *New York Times* praised the film, noting that while its rural mountain setting is powerful, it is Lawrence's portrayal of Ree Dolly that stands out. "Its setting is finally subordinate to the main character, as memorable and vivid a heroine as you are likely to see on screen this season," he notes.

Scott wrote that Lawrence was key to the film, and that the audience would have difficulty not relating to the perilous situation in which she and her siblings find themselves. "Anxious sympathy for this young woman in peril—at 17, barely more than a child herself and forced to respond to challenges that would terrify most adults—is the prevailing emotion you are likely to feel when watching 'Winter's Bone.' It is straightforward and suspenseful but also surprising and subtle."[1]

The *New Yorker*, too, gave the movie a thumbs-up. Reviewer David Denby was impressed with Lawrence's performance:

> Some of [the cast] are local people, but the main roles are taken by professional actors, including Jennifer Lawrence, who has flowing blond hair, lidless blue eyes, and a full mouth. Her Ree is the head of a household, a womanly girl with no time for her own pleasure, and Lawrence establishes the character's authority right away, with a level stare and an unhurried voice that suggest heavy lifting from an early age. The movie would be unimaginable with anyone less charismatic playing Ree.[2]

A.O. Scott. "Where Life Is Cold, and Kin Are Cruel." *New York Times*, June 11, 2010. www.nytimes.com/2010/06/11/movies/11winter.html?_r=0.

David Denby. "Thrills and Chills." *New Yorker*, July 5, 2010. www.newyorker.com/magazine/2010/07/05/thrills-and-chills.

Swan, and *True Grit*. John Hawkes was nominated for Best Supporting Actor. And among the nominees for Best Actress was Jennifer Lawrence.

The word *shocked*, if used to describe Lawrence's reaction to her nomination, would have been an understatement. "Someone snapped a photo of her and her family just as her name was being read," reports Josh Eells of *Rolling Stone*. "The look on her face, she said, was 'like I'm being sent off to jail.'"[71] Her friend Zoe Kravitz says she loved teasing Lawrence about how unlikely she was to win: "You're up against Natalie Portman [star of *The Black Swan*], you don't stand a chance," Kravitz told her; to which Lawrence replied, "You're right, I don't!"[72]

Oscars in Perspective

When the big night arrived, Lawrence was thrilled to walk the red carpet wearing a simple Calvin Klein tank dress in bright red and happily chatting with reporters along the way. And true to form, she was unabashedly honest with reporters—this time about the fact that she had ignored her hairstylist's advice to eat lightly before the awards ceremony. "Fifteen minutes before, the guy doing my hair goes, 'If you can get a salad, get a salad.' I said, 'I'm getting a Philly cheesesteak.'"[73]

She recalled later how much fun the experience was. "I was really excited because [one of my favorite bands] Florence and the Machine was playing. I really remember that performance really well. It was great. I loved being able to sit next to my dad. We just kept looking at each other like, 'I can't believe this is happening.'"[74]

As it turned out, Lawrence did not win. Natalie Portman took the award for Best Actress for her work in *Black Swan*, a psychological thriller that takes place in the world of ballet. Lawrence was content to be able to display what she called her loser's face, which she had practiced in front of the mirror. But while she was disappointed, she had her family there to keep reminding her of the positive things she had accomplished. Her mother told one reporter that their view of their daughter's career is not measured by the awards she wins: "The thing we're most proud

Jennifer Lawrence arrives at the 2011 Academy Awards ceremony. She says she enjoyed her first attendance at the event, even though she lost.

of is when we go on set with these people who are around her 18 hours a day. They see who she really is—they say she's gracious, down-to-earth."[75]

Her father agrees. "The one thing I will say, when I go on a set, the hair and makeup people always come up to me and say she's such a nice girl, so respectful. And I kid her and say, 'If I ever come and don't hear that, we'll have some real problems.' But so far, so good."[76]

The Beaver

In the months following the Academy Awards, *Winter's Bone* got a second predictable boost in attendance from its Oscar recognition, but *The Beaver*, another indie film that Lawrence had made in 2009, was having disappointing results at the box office. The opening of the film had been delayed almost two years.

Unlike many independent films, whose casts are composed of largely unknown actors, *The Beaver* boasted two well-known Hollywood stars: Mel Gibson and Jodie Foster. Foster also directed the film. Gibson plays Walter Black, a toy company executive battling depression, whose wife, Meredith (played by Foster), has kicked him out of the house. Walter finds it difficult to talk directly with his family and realizes that the only way he can communicate with his wife and two sons is by using a beaver hand puppet. Lawrence plays Norah, a friend of Walter and Meredith's elder son, Porter, played by Anton Yelchin.

Jennifer Lawrence and Anton Yelchin appear in 2011 film **The Beaver.** *Although the film was a disappointment at the box office, Lawrence's career would soon take off in Hollywood.*

Unfortunately, Gibson had real-life personal problems that had become very public prior to the scheduled opening of *The Beaver*. Just as the filming was ending, he was arrested for battering and verbally abusing his ex-girlfriend, against whom he had already made racist threats. He pleaded no contest and was sentenced to three years' probation. Gibson already had damaged his reputation in 2006 after a much-publicized anti-Semitic rant against police officers who had stopped him for drunk driving.

It was clear that news stories of Gibson's recent actions were likely to keep people away from the new film. To let the negative talk about Gibson simmer down, Foster and the film's distributors felt it was best to delay the premiere of *The Beaver*; however, even with the delay, the film attracted a far smaller audience than hoped when it finally opened in May 2011.

And though the box office results for *The Beaver* were disappointing, Lawrence had no time to dwell on it. She was busy preparing for a kind of film she had never done before: a big Hollywood movie that was virtually guaranteed to be a blockbuster—and she would do it all while painted bright blue.

Chapter 4

Hungry for More

Soon after the filming of *Winter's Bone* was completed, in June 2010, Lawrence's agents talked with her about broadening her career. Many of the roles she had played recently —especially in *Winter's Bone*, *The Poker House*, and *The Burning Plain*—had been gritty and demanding, showing off her tough, strong side.

But her agents believed it was important to show that she could be softer, glamorous, and more vulnerable, too. If she did not show that side of herself, there was a danger she would be typecast—only being offered a specific type of role—which would limit her career.

Lawrence told a reporter:

I'm happy that [indies] are the movies I'm breaking out in. . . . It's the same reason I don't wear low-cut shirts and short shorts. I don't want to be remembered as the girl with great boobs. I have a brain, I believe I have talent, and that's what I want to break me out. So, now that those were my first three movies, I feel like I can move on.[77]

One dramatic departure for Lawrence was doing a photo shoot for *Esquire*, a men's magazine. She agreed with her agent that it was a good way to shake things up, because appearing in a number of photographs—including one in which she was wearing a sexy swimsuit—was the polar opposite of the look she had sported in her indie movies.

Meeting a Role Model

While the box office profits of *The Beaver* were disappointing, Lawrence still counted making the film as a valuable experience—especially getting to know Jodie Foster. Lawrence later reflected on how important it was to her to work with someone like Foster, who is not only extremely talented and smart but also someone who carries herself as a normal, everyday person.

"She's brilliant," Lawrence told reporter Marlowe Stern. "She has the mind of five men and she's the most normal person I've met since I've been doing this. It's as if someone forgot to tell her she's famous; she has no idea. She's just a mom. She's nice, smart, and is a calming presence on the set. She never got too excited or too upset about something. She's very level."

Lawrence also said that the two of them bonded because their careers were somewhat similar. Like Lawrence, Foster had begun acting as a child. They also have similar views about movies and acting. She said later that both of them walked away from their first meeting thinking that they had just met someone that reminded them of themselves.

Quoted in Marlowe Stern. "Jennifer Lawrence Is the Breakout Star of *Winter's Bone!*" *Manhattan Movie Magazine*, June 12, 2010. www.manhattanmoviemag.com/interviews /jennifer-lawrence-is-the-breakout-star-of-winter%E2%80%99s-bone.html.

A Different Sort of Movie

Late in 2010, Lawrence headed to London to audition for an upcoming movie called *X-Men: First Class*. It was a different sort of movie than the ones she had done so far—a movie made by a large Hollywood studio. The movie is a prequel to the previous movies in the series, showing audiences how the X-Men got their start. The stories and characters are based on popular Marvel comic books. Lawrence had not seen the previous movies, but after watching them on DVD, she was very enthusiastic about auditioning.

The X-Men are humans born with various mutations that have endowed them with certain abilities that other humans do not possess. These abilities range from Wolverine's power to heal himself immediately from any injury or ailment, to that of Rogue, a mutant who can absorb or remove the strength or mutant powers from anyone she touches. According to the stories, the X-Men are considered the next step in human evolution.

The part for which Lawrence was auditioning was Mystique, a mutant whose real name is Raven Darkholme. Mystique's special power is to shape-shift, that is, to take on the appearance of any other person she chooses. The character of Mystique had been played in previous movies by Rebecca Romijn, but in this movie, Mystique and the other members of the X-Men team had to be played by younger actors, since it was a prequel—taking place in the 1960s during the Cold War between the United States and the Soviet Union.

Some Doubts

Auditioning for a part in an X-Men film was about as radical a change as it was possible to make from the gritty independent films that Lawrence had previously made. *X-Men: First Class* was almost certain to become a blockbuster, since the other films in the series had done extremely well at the box office. And that made it very likely that there would be sequels that she would be expected to be part of.

Lawrence had some doubts about committing herself to something that might last for years, as she later explained to one reporter:

It's hard to talk about a movie to do when there are sequels, and you haven't read the script because, what if I hate the script and I have to make it three times? So I think the sequels were the biggest thing for me, because I was thinking that I have no idea where I'm going to be in my life when these new movies come out. I don't know what kind of

things I'm going to be doing. Am I going to regret this decision I made when I was 20? So I wanted to really think about it."[78]

Lawrence realized later that she had made a mistake by auditioning for *X-Men: First Class* without knowing anything about the previous X-Men movies. In retrospect, she was astonished that the movie's director had bothered to ask her back for more auditions since she believed that she had been portraying Mystique all wrong:

I am ashamed to say I auditioned three times before I even watched any of the movies. And then after I watched the

The cast of the film X-Men: First Class includes (from left) Caleb Landry Jones, Michael Fassbender, Jennifer Lawrence, Rose Byrne, Nicholas Hoult, James McAvoy, and Lucas Till.

movies, I was like, "Oh my God, I've been doing it all wrong, why are they calling me back?" I was doing [Mystique] all sweet and naïve. I saw Rebecca Romijn [the original Mystique], and she's sultry and mean. I know this is an origin story, but I was definitely doing it all wrong.[79]

Lawrence, however, got excited when she learned that the movie's leading men were two actors she greatly admired: Michael Fassbender (as Magneto, one of the mutants) and James McAvoy (as Professor Xavier, who trains the mutants to use their powers more effectively). When she had an opportunity to read through the script, she was highly impressed. Finally, as if working with actors she loved on a movie with a great script were not enough, she was thrilled that the movie would be filmed in London. That sealed the deal: She would definitely play Mystique.

Becoming Mystique

One of the strangest aspects of her role as Mystique was the costume—or actually, the lack of one. Mystique is blue and scaly. It was decided that rather than have Lawrence wear a skin-tight blue bodysuit, she would be naked but painted blue, with

To appear in her character Mystique's natural state in
X-Men: First Class, Jennifer Lawrence's intricate make-up
took six to eight hours to apply each day, starting at 4 A.M.

scales added in strategic places to preserve modesty. The process
was tedious and sometimes painful.

Each day that she filmed her scenes, makeup artists went
through the meticulous process of transforming her into Mystique. The process took between six and eight hours to complete. She would have to arrive at 4 A.M. so that she would be
"in costume" by the time the directors were ready to shoot her
scenes. Her whole body would be shaved and then rubbed
down with alcohol to dry it off. Five coats of paint coated every
inch of her body, and then the makeup artists added scales made
of silicone. It was often uncomfortable, for her skin reacted to
the chemicals in the paint, which caused blisters and burns and
even left scars. To complete her metamorphosis into Mystique,

her eyes were turned yellow by means of bright yellow contact lenses.

During the hours-long process of being airbrushed with layers of blue paint or having scales applied, Lawrence was unable to lie down or sit in a comfortable chair. She had a choice between standing up the whole time, or leaning back on what was basically a narrow bicycle seat. But while the process was long and uncomfortable, she said she and her makeup artist friends killed time by watching episodes of TV shows such as *Sex and the City*.

The blue paint had a strange odor—which grew stronger with each layer—and Lawrence joked that her character should be called Mystink instead of Mystique. Luckily, however, in most of her scenes she was Mystique's alter ego, Raven Darkholme, so she had to endure the body-painting ordeal only eight days. She did complain that when the filming was over and she was moving out of her apartment in London, she was denied her damage deposit because the bathtub had vivid blue stains that even a good scrubbing could not remove.

Similarities and Differences

Lawrence discovered that working on *X-Men* and working on indie films such as *Winter's Bone* or *The Burning Plain* were immensely different experiences. The budget was one obvious difference. *Winter's Bone* had a total budget of $2 million and was shot in twenty-six days, while *X-Men: First Class* began with an operating budget of more than $120 million for 100 days of filming.

Another difference between the two films was evident to Lawrence on the first day of filming *X-Men: First Class*: The size of the production team was nearly three times that of *Winter's Bone*. One of things that most fascinated Lawrence was that there was actually a member of the staff whose job it was to write down a detailed, minute-to-minute log of Lawrence's daily routine on the set. Lawrence later told a reporter about one morning when one of the makeup staff came in and proudly showed off her engagement ring to Lawrence. As the two jumped up and down, crying with joy, that moment was actually included in Lawrence's log. It read: "Three minutes, 19 seconds—cries and shaved." Lawrence still laughs about it. "They gave me the piece of paper so I could frame it,"[80] she says.

Even with such excesses, Lawrence said that many people might be surprised to know that there were more similarities than differences in the two different sorts of movies. "It's all film-making," she says. "The behind-the-scenes is always different: You have a bigger trailer, there's better food. Things like that. I still do the movies for the same reasons. I still love the script, I love the director, I love the character [I play] and the other actors involved. So all of the reasons why I was there, they were all the same. It's kind of like camping versus going to a resort. They're both fun; they're just different kinds of fun."[81]

The Role of a Lifetime

Soon after the filming of *X-Men* was finished, the breaking news from Hollywood was that the *Hunger Games* books by Suzanne Collins were to be made into a series of movies. Collins's books, aimed at a young adult audience, had been wildly popular, selling more than 11 million copies since the first in the series was published in 2008. Not surprisingly, the announcement that the first of the three books was to be turned into a film was met with a great deal of excitement.

The *Hunger Games* books are set in a bleak, postapocalyptic future in the nation of Panem, built on the ruins of what was once North America. Panem is split into twelve districts and the Capitol, which controls the districts. People in the districts are poor and hungry and have to hunt for their food, while the Capitol is rich and technologically advanced. As a punishment for a revolt years before by the districts against the Capitol, Panem's leaders organized a violent, televised competition between districts called the Hunger Games. The names of two representatives (called Tributes), a boy and a girl between the ages of twelve and eighteen, are drawn from each district. The Tributes must fight each other to the death. The last Tribute left alive is declared the winner, and as a reward, his or her district

More than fifty accomplished actresses auditioned for the highly coveted role of Katniss Everdeen in **The Hunger Games.**

is given many gifts—especially food, which is in huge demand throughout Panem.

In March 2011 Lawrence auditioned for the part of the books' narrator and protagonist, sixteen-year-old Katniss Everdeen. She was not alone—in fact, more than fifty accomplished actresses had their hearts set on snagging the role. Lawrence was aware that she was up against some formidable young talents, including Abigail Breslin, who had garnered an Oscar nomination for her supporting role in the hit movie *Little Miss Sunshine*, and Hailee Steinfeld, who had recently received an Oscar nomination for her role in *True Grit*.

An Amazing Audition

The director of the movie, Gary Ross, had gained fame for writing the screenplays for *Pleasantville* and *Seabiscuit*, as well as directing and producing them (the latter was nominated for the Academy Award for Best Picture in 2003). Ross and producer Nina Jacobson decided to make their decision about who should play Katniss on the basis of one important scene—that in which Katniss is heading off for the Hunger Games and is saying good-bye to her twelve-year-old sister, Primrose. It is a powerfully emotional scene, as both girls realize that it is likely they will never see one another again.

Ross admits that he was astonished at what Lawrence did with her character in that scene. "I got choked up," he says. "You only see that kind of talent once in a generation—that kind of intensity and emotional power. If you don't find the right performer, you don't have the movie. So I felt like, 'Now I can make the movie.'"[82]

Jacobson agrees, saying it was impossible to not tear up while Lawrence was talking to Primrose. "In her audition, Jen stole the role. There was instant power, intensity and certainty in her performance. Some people can be fierce and others can be tender, but Jen is both."[83]

A Good Choice?

But while Lawrence was thrilled that she had been chosen to play Katniss, there were howls of protest from many fans of the books when her name was announced as the lead in the upcoming film. Some complained that she was a poor choice because she was too old (Katniss was sixteen in the first book, and Lawrence was twenty when she filmed the first movie in the series). Others said she was too glamorous.

Lawrence understood the complaints because she knew very well that readers are frequently very protective of the books they love and resent an actor who does not seem to fit what they imagined he or she would look like. She herself admits that when she heard that *The Hunger Games* were going to be

A Welcome Voice of Support

Many fans of the *The Hunger Games* books were highly critical of the casting of Lawrence to play Katniss. As the Internet sites buzzed with complaints about how she was too blonde or too old or too glamorous, it was clear that the negative chatter was not going to go away.

Finally, the one thing that eased fans' doubts about Lawrence's playing the role of Katniss was the sincere, full-throated support of Lawrence by *Hunger Games* author Suzanne Collins herself. In a statement to *Entertainment Weekly*, Collins explained how vitally important it was to her that the actress that would play Katniss had to match up with how she had written the character in the book:

> As the author, I went into the casting process with a certain degree of trepidation. Believing your heroine can make the leap from the relative safety of the page to the flesh-and-bones reality of the screen is something of a creative act of faith. But after watching dozens of auditions by a group of very fine young actresses, I felt there was only one who truly captured the character I wrote in the book. And I'm thrilled to say that Jennifer Lawrence has accepted the role . . . . Jennifer's just an incredible actress. So powerful, vulnerable, beautiful, unforgiving and brave. I never thought we'd find somebody this amazing for the role. And I can't wait for everyone to see her play it.

Quoted in Darren Franich. 'Hunger Games': Suzanne Collins Talks Jennifer Lawrence as Katniss." *Entertainment Weekly*, March 21, 2011. http://insidemovies.ew.com/2011/03/21 /hunger-games-suzanne-collins-jennifer-lawrence.

made into movies, she was disappointed. "I didn't hear about the movie and go, 'Oh boy, I want to join in,'" she recalls. "I thought, 'Great, they're going to ruin another great book series with a movie.'"[84]

But after she had met with Ross and learned what he was planning to do, she quickly changed her mind. "Everything he had to say about the characters, the relationships, and about Suzanne's work was incredible," she says. "I realized that [no one involved in the movie] was interested in being part of a watered-down version. I knew it was going to be an incredible film."[85]

Becoming Katniss

As with most of her previous films, Lawrence had a lot of preparation to do before she began filming, and most of that preparation was physical. Katniss was put through a series of difficult tasks during the Hunger Games, and Lawrence needed to be in

Jennifer Lawrence endured intense training to learn archery for her role in **The Hunger Games.**

top physical condition. She learned rock climbing and hand-to-hand combat. She did yoga and ran hour-long speed drills on a track each day. Ross stressed to her trainer that while she did not need to appear gaunt for the part, her appearance needed to remind people that she—like the others in her district—was hungry.

But the most intense and difficult training Lawrence endured was learning archery. Ross had hired a four-time Olympic archer from eastern Europe to teach her how to skillfully handle a bow and arrow—something she found difficult at first. Finally, her archery teacher made her angry by calling her "helpless," so she gritted her teeth, fired, and hit the bull's-eye.

While her training was often grueling, Lawrence was in such good condition afterward that she was able to do many of her own stunts for the movie—even though she credits her stunt double for the most difficult ones. "I did as many stunts as I could," she told one reporter, but "the studio wasn't too big on having their lead actress doing insane stunts at the beginning of a franchise. So I had a wonderful stunt girl to fall out of trees for me and roll down mountains."[86]

Bears, Turkeys, and New Friends

The filming lasted for four months in the woods of North Carolina. It was hard work but also a great deal of fun. Lawrence and her fellow cast members enjoyed seeing the baby bears that frequently wandered onto the movie set. Wild turkeys also flocked to the set, and one of the assistant directors was given the job of trying (usually without success) to scare them away.

Lawrence thoroughly enjoyed getting to know the cast, and the feeling seemed to be mutual. Josh Hutcherson, who plays Peeta, Katniss's love interest in the movie, became a close friend. In fact, they were such good friends that it was hard to act the required sexual tension in their movie scenes. "The problem is that Josh and me, our chemistry is like a brother and a sister, like an annoying brother and sister," Lawrence explains. "We'd be fighting over whose face is on the $10 bill. We'd have huge fights, screaming at each other, and then we'd be doing weird giggling, and playing like we're cats. It wasn't a chemistry you hope to find between two lovers."[87]

She also enjoyed working with Woody Harrelson, who plays the part of Haymitch Abernathy, a former champion of the Hunger Games. Harrelson was delighted with the young actress and her oddball sense of humor, saying later that he found it charming that she was so unlike many Hollywood actresses. "Jennifer doesn't have a trace of arrogance," he says. "She's not trying to put on any airs or be anyone she's not. She's the real deal. She's just this frickin' amazing gal from Kentucky who hit it big."[88]

Silver Linings Playbook

Soon after she finished filming *The Hunger Games*, Lawrence was cast in an independent film called *Silver Linings Playbook*. Filmed in Pennsylvania in late 2011 and directed by David O. Russell, the film tells the story of Pat, a man who has been in a psychiatric hospital for bipolar disorder. Pat has become estranged from his wife because of his condition, but after he is released from the hospital, he hopes to get back together with her. The only woman who seems able to relate to him, however, is an eccentric young woman named Tiffany, who also has a troubled past.

Bradley Cooper was cast as Pat, but the part of Tiffany was unsettled. Russell had originally cast Anne Hathaway for the part, but she eventually declined because of schedule conflicts. After that, there was a rather large group of actresses that were considered to play Tiffany, including Rachel McAdams, who had won an MTV Award for *Mean Girls* and had starred in *The Notebook*; Rooney Mara, who had starred in *The Social Network* and *The Girl with the Dragon Tattoo*; and superstar Angelina Jolie. But even though they are all extremely talented, Russell was not sure that any of them was right for the part of Tiffany.

Finally, he scheduled an audition for Lawrence, who was back in Louisville spending time with her parents. Lawrence did a reading for Russell via Skype, and the director was completely overwhelmed with her long-distance performance. "We went,

Jennifer Lawrence and Bradley Cooper perform in a scene of the 2013 film Silver Linings Playbook. Lawrence says Cooper was fun to work with on the set.

'Oh my God, who is this person?'," he recalled later to the *Hollywood Reporter*. "We didn't know she had all that in her."[89] Not surprisingly, she got the part.

A Surprising Request

Lawrence thoroughly enjoyed filming *Silver Linings Playbook*. Besides being challenged to portray such a complex character as Tiffany, she was pleasantly surprised by the openness of the other actors on the set. She found Bradley Cooper to be fun

Robert De Niro (left) and Bradley Cooper—Jennifer Lawrence's co-stars in Silver Linings Playbook—*and David O. Russell, the director, attend the movie's premier at the 2012 Toronto Film Festival, in Ontario, Canada.*

to hang around with on the set but was positively in awe of working with Robert De Niro—widely considered to be one of the greatest actors of all time. In fact, on one afternoon, De Niro's presence on the set became a watershed moment in her own career.

It began with Lawrence remembering that De Niro was her father's favorite actor. She had been thinking how excited her father would be to get De Niro's autograph; however, as she recalls to *Rolling Stone* reporter Josh Eells, she was not sure how to ask De Niro and had been dithering about it for weeks. "I was in my trailer, freaking out," she says. "I didn't want to bug him."[90]

She had been sitting for a long time, wondering whether she should ask De Niro or whether it was too odd a request, when she heard a knock on her trailer door. It was De Niro's personal assistant, who asked, "Would you mind autographing a couple of things for Bob?"[91] If being asked for an autograph by Robert De Niro was a measure of Hollywood success, Lawrence felt she had truly arrived.

Chapter 5

Oscar and Beyond

N ot only did *Silver Linings Playbook* do well at the box office but it also received eight Oscar nominations—including Best Picture, Best Director, Best Actor, and Best Actress. Lawrence had been nominated before for *Winter's Bone* and knew very well that actually winning the Oscar was far from a given. Even so, the experience for Lawrence and her family was thrilling.

The event actually begins weeks before the night of the Oscars ceremony, because of the number of pre-Oscar interviews, appearances, and promotional photo shoots in which the nominees are expected to take part. For Lawrence, wardrobe people were in and out of the house, as were stylists, manicurists, makeup artists, and teams that came in bearing a glittering assortment of jewelry. "I call it the pit crew," her father says. "They just take over the house, so I just stay out of the way."[92]

The Oscars ceremony itself was exciting for the Lawrence family. Brother Ben recalls how he, his brother, and their parents rotated where they were sitting. It was Lawrence's mother, Karen, however, who was sitting next to her when her name was announced as the winner. And though it was embarrassing, the stumble on the stairs did not overshadow the joyful experience for her and her family.

In winning the Oscar for Best Actress, Lawrence became the "new biggest thing" in show business. Magazines wanted her face on their covers, television hosts such as David Letterman and Jimmy Fallon scrambled to book her for guest appearances

Staying Loose

David O. Russell, who directed Lawrence in *Silver Linings Playbook*, agrees that one of her strengths as an actress is her ability to stay relaxed and loose when she is not involved in a scene. He remembers thinking that Lawrence was fooling around on the set between takes, instead of watching what was going on with her fellow actors:

> I remember Bradley Cooper and I saying, "Is this kid even paying attention?" Because she's goofing around or eating my potato chips or making fart jokes. And then all of a sudden, she comes in, and *bam!* She's like a lot of great athletes. You see that they stay loose, and that's how they can be so in-the-moment while under enormous amounts of pressure. If there's two minutes left in the game, they can come in and do something extraordinary because their jaw is not getting clenched. Jen stays loose. And then she hits a three-point-shot from some ridiculous distance and we all just look at each other and go, "Wow."

Quoted in Jonathan Van Meter. *"The Hunger Games'* Jennifer Lawrence Covers the September Issue." *Vogue*, August 12, 2013. www.vogue.com/865209/star-quality-jennifer-lawrence-hunger-games.

on their programs, and the French luxury goods company Dior signed her to do fashion ads.

As Lawrence's name has become increasingly famous in Hollywood, critics and fans have been interested in how Lawrence has achieved so much acting success at such a young age. In fact, she is the youngest person in the history of the Academy Awards to have received two leading-actor nominations. Not surprisingly, many wonder how such a young, virtually untrained actress has been so effective in such a wide variety of roles.

The *Hunger Games* director Gary Ross says that even after working with her, he continues to be amazed at how talented she is: "I've worked with some amazing actors, and I've never seen anyone with more raw talent. There's a reservoir of emotional power in her that's sort of stunning. Sometimes I'd say to her, 'Where did you come from?' And she'd say, 'You know, I really don't know.'"[93]

The Method to Her Success

Lawrence herself says that she has always loved watching people—how they react in various situations. Being observant has helped her, she says, when she is playing a role. She also says that she tries to stay relaxed, because she has learned that when she tries too hard or becomes stressed, her acting suffers. "To you, it looks emotionally straining, but I don't get emotionally drained, because I don't invest any of my real emotions. I don't even take it to craft services [the snack tables set up for cast and crew on set]."[94]

Lawrence remembers having doubts about her acting ability when she was on the set of *The Hunger Games*. Woody Harrelson was watching her work and gave her what he intended as a compliment, remarking that watching her work made him feel as though he actually was working too hard. Harrelson's comment stuck with her, however, and she began wondering if she was somehow not practicing or working as hard as she should be. After a few days she talked to her father about it. "I said, 'Is this bad? Do I need to be memorizing more, or saying my lines out loud?' And my dad just went, 'It ain't broke. Don't fix it.'"[95]

"I like to do as little work as possible, definitely," she explains. "I think it makes it more natural and more real. There are times when I've been doing a scene, and we've gone for five or six takes, and I'm just dead. I've memorized what I'm saying, I've memorized what my co-star is saying, and it's not real anymore."[96] She explains that while it may seem like bragging, she feels that acting is simply something that comes easily to her. "Some people are doctors, and doing surgery comes easy to them. Some writers, the words just fly. I have a friend who can write the most beautiful song that will break your heart in 25 minutes. There are certain things that people are just wired for. And for me, acting is one of those things. I understand it—and that's good, because it's pretty much the only thing in the entire world that I do understand."[97]

The Quote Machine

Lawrence's performances in both the *X-Men* and *Hunger Games* movies—in addition to her Oscar win in *Silver Linings Playbook*—generated a whirlwind of excitement around her as she became recognizable and much sought-after for television and print interviews. The press loved her—sometimes referring to her as a "quote machine" because she was candid and

Jennifer Lawrence signs autographs following an appearance on the **Late Show with David Letterman** *in 2012. After her Oscar win, she was in high demand for talk shows and endorsements.*

funny, and had the rare Hollywood trait of being able to laugh at herself. And for that reason alone, any journalist who was able to line up an interview with Jennifer Lawrence was considered very lucky indeed.

Initially, she enjoyed the opportunity to wisecrack with reporters but soon learned that her candor could sometimes backfire. One such instance happened after an interview with *Rolling Stone* magazine, during which she made fun of her Kentucky upbringing. "Little redneck things still come out," she told the reporter. "I'm attracted to my brother. Stuff like that."[98]

Of course, she meant the comment as a joke, but her family was outraged—especially after the story went viral. "I was actually cracking up about that," she said later, "though I was the only one. My mom was so mad. 'Jen! This is not funny! You cannot laugh at this!' And I was like, 'Mom, this is my first scandal, and it's hilarious.'"[99]

She admits, however, that there are times when her candor with the press can be a problem. "I never know what's going to come out of my mouth, and it's horrible. I don't find it positive in any way. When I get older, I'll be more mature and poised. And I'll have control over my mouth. One day, I'm going to grow up. . . . When we leave [this interview] I'm going to have a knot in my stomach," she told the reporter. "I'm going to be like, 'Oh, did I say something wrong? I'm going to get in trouble!'"[100]

But while her family believes she crosses the line too frequently, many of her coworkers find her candor a breath of fresh air in an industry that tends to be scripted and phony. Woody Harrelson adores her for her wit and humor, and Jodie Foster, who directed *The Beaver*, hopes she never loses that spontaneity, saying, "That's one of the things I love about her the most—her rapid-fire teenage-boy-humor brain."[101]

The Downside of Being Famous

While fame and success have some obvious advantages, they also have a price. One of the hardest things Lawrence has had to get used to as her fame has grown is the associated lack of

Jennifer Lawrence is followed by mob of photographers—one of the downsides of being a major celebrity—at the Los Angeles International Airport in 2013.

privacy. Everywhere she goes, people recognize her—something that had never happened to her before. *Silver Linings Playbook* director David O. Russell says he witnessed her celebrity status blossom before his eyes:

When she first showed up on the set of *Silver Linings*, she was asking Bradley Cooper and Robert De Niro what it's like to have people come up to you on the street. That wasn't really happening to her. People didn't really know who she was. But by the time the film was released and we did an event in Santa Barbara, it was like being at a Beatles concert. There were thousands of screaming people. It was mind-blowing.[102]

But while at first the recognition was exciting and fun, Lawrence soon realized that she was no longer living her life on her own terms. Instead, she found herself being followed by photographers wherever she went—whether to a friend's house, on a date with a boyfriend, or just going out for a morning run to get coffee.

"I'm Kind of Going Through a Meltdown"

Lawrence knows that complaining about her lack of privacy may sound ungrateful, and she realizes that people have little sympathy for celebrities who grumble about being famous. But it is an odd feeling, she says, that every detail of her life is fair game for the press, or that every time she gets into a car to go somewhere, reporters and photographers consider it an opportunity to follow her.

She is uncomfortable that the world feels entitled to know everything about her, she says, even when she is spending time with family. And what bothers her most is that she cannot ask for privacy without sounding ungrateful, for she understands that many people would love to be in her shoes.

She admits that she tends to get very emotional about the invasiveness of paparazzi, but it has been very upsetting. The world, she says, seems to think that every aspect of her life should be public—not only the movies she is working on but also the family members and friends with whom she spends time.

As she told Jonathan Van Meter of *Vogue*, most people would be protected from being stalked by legions of reporters and photographers:

Time for a Fan

Some of Lawrence's most generous acts have been with people she does not even know. For instance, at the premiere of *The Hunger Games: Catching Fire* in London in November 2013, she was walking on the red carpet when she noticed a young girl in a wheelchair, quietly crying.

Lawrence veered off the red carpet and quickly walked over to the girl, bent down, gave her a hug, and began talking with her. The girl, fifteen-year-old Jessica Hambly, suffers from a rare disease that weakens the heart, lungs, and joints of her body. A huge fan of Suzanne Collins's books, as well as of Lawrence herself, Jessica had been given a chance to attend the film's premiere because of an organization in Britain called Starlight, which is similar to the Make-a-Wish Foundation in the United States. Jessica was overcome with emotion when she spotted Lawrence, her favorite actress. Lawrence spoke to Jessica's mother for several minutes and posed for photos with the young girl.

Afterward, Lawrence explained to reporters that it made her proud to be playing a character that resonates with fans like Jessica. "Growing up I didn't have a female hero the way that Katniss is," she told reporters. "I think she's a wonderful role model for young girls. I'm happy that they have a character like that."

Quoted in Chiderah Monde. "Jennifer Lawrence Leaves 'Hunger Games: Catching Fire' Red Carpet to Comfort Crying Girl in Wheelchair." *New York Daily News*, November 12, 2013. www.nydailynews.com/entertainment/gossip/jennifer-lawrence-comforts-crying -girl-wheelchair-article-1.1514221#ixzz3BLLcHV00.

If I were just your average 23-year-old girl and I called the police to say that there were strange men sleeping on my lawn and following me to Starbucks, they would leap into action. But because I am a famous person, "well, sorry ma'am, there's nothing we can do." It makes no sense. . . . I am just not OK with it. It's as simple as that. I am just a normal girl and a human being, and I haven't been in this long enough to feel like this is my new normal. I'm not going to find peace with it.[103]

Gary Lawrence, her father, is even more outspoken. He says that it shocks him to see the way paparazzi yell insults at her and other celebrities, shoving and putting cameras in their faces, hoping to get a photo showing their reaction. He worries that his daughter—or any other celebrity—could be hurt.

Working Hard

The next project Lawrence turned to after finishing *The Hunger Games: Catching Fire* was the 2013 film *American Hustle*, in which she joined *Silver Linings Playbook* castmate Bradley Cooper, as well as Amy Adams and Christian Bale. The story takes place during the FBI's ABSCAM operation of the late 1970s and early 1980s, which eventually uncovered corruption among several members of Congress. Lawrence plays Rosalyn, the wife of Bale's character.

The movie drew mostly rave reviews, such as that of the website Rotten Tomatoes, which called *American Hustle* "riotously funny and impeccably cast."[104] Richard Roeper, film critic of the *Chicago Sun-Times*, raved, "*American Hustle* is the best time I've had at the movies all year, a movie so perfectly executed, such wall-to-wall fun, so filled with the joy of expert filmmaking on every level I can't imagine anyone who loves movies not loving THIS movie."[105] The film was nominated for numerous Academy Awards, including Best Supporting Actress for Lawrence, but unfortunately failed to win any.

In 2014, Lawrence reprised her role as Mystique in *X-Men: Days of Future Past*. The world premiere of the much-anticipated movie took place in New York on May 10, 2014, and the reviews were very positive. "The most ambitious and ingenious of the long-running series, *X-Men: Days of Future Past* keeps the key crew of mutants busier than ever," wrote Claudia Puig of *USA Today*. "Between globe-hopping, time-traveling and employing their various powers early and often, these superhuman folks are non-stop in this riveting sequel."[106]

Jennifer Lawrence and Amy Adams perform in scene from American Hustle. *The film earned mostly rave reviews and received several Academy Award nominations, including Best Supporting Actress for Lawrence.*

Tom Riordan, a Chicago drama teacher, was especially impressed with Lawrence's work in *X-Men: Days of Future Past.* "She was virtually the thread that connected this movie," he says. "I'm constantly amazed at the way she can be different in each and every movie she appears in. It's not that she's playing different roles—of course she is—but she appears to be drawing from a new wellspring of emotions each time. She's got so many layers, you don't know what to expect next—and I think that makes her audience want to keep watching."[107]

Staying Normal

Given the legions of paparazzi and adoring fans who follow Lawrence, her parents say that their greatest hope for their daughter is that she can remain grounded even as her fame

Saved by a Castmate!

Of the many relationships Lawrence has forged with actors she has worked with, one of the strongest is her friendship with Woody Harrelson, who appeared with her in *The Hunger Games* movies. Lawrence not only relished his sense of humor on the set but also says that she owes him for actually saving her life.

It happened on the set of *The Hunger Games: Mockingjay—Part 2*. According to a member of the film crew, Lawrence began choking after swallowing several of the daily vitamins she takes—and if it had not been for quick thinking on the part of Harrelson, she may have choked to death. The crew member recounts the story:

> Jennifer had just downed a handful of her daily vitamins, swallowing them with water, but one got caught in her throat. Suddenly she started gagging, gasping, pointing at her throat as her face turned bright red. Everyone around her froze, not knowing what to do. But when a crew person screamed, "Help," Woody quickly ran up behind Jennifer and gave her a swift, hard slap on the back. When that didn't help, he wrapped his powerful arms just under her chest, gave two quick, strong squeezes, and the vitamin popped out of her mouth.

> Afterward, Lawrence hugged him and said, "Ohmigod, you literally just saved my life. I really couldn't breathe . . . . I really thought I was gonna die right here. That was the scariest thing ever!"

Quoted in Aqib Mansoor, "Woody Harrelson Saved Jennifer Lawrence Life from Choking." Trendy Matters, April 7, 2014. http://trendymatter.com/woody-harrelson-saved-jennifer-lawrence-life-chocking.

and success continue to grow. So far, her mother says, it appears that she is the same old Jennifer when she comes home to visit. For example, her mother says that for a young woman making millions of dollars, her daughter does not act wealthy

—preferring to be just the same with her family as she has always been.

Her mother says that Jennifer was able to choose virtually any new car to drive—free of charge—because companies offer to foot the bill simply for the publicity. But instead of choosing a flashy sports car or huge luxury SUV, Lawrence drives a Chevy Volt. "I don't even think she thinks about money," says Karen Lawrence. "When she's home, she'll say, 'Dad, can I have $20 bucks to go to the movies?' He usually treats for dinner when we're out because that's what we would normally do. She wants to be treated like everyone else."[108]

According to her aunt, Cindy Miller, Jennifer's taste buds have not matured as rapidly as her career has grown. "The last time she came home, I'll never forget," says Miller. "Jennifer called Karen from the airport and said, 'Hi Mom! All I want are Ramen noodles and sugar pops, or some sugary cereal—Cap'n Crunch!'—that's what she wanted."[109]

"It'll Never Happen to Me Again"

Even more than the lack of privacy, one of the issues about which Lawrence has been very outspoken has been the pressure on girls and young women to be thin. Nowhere is this pressure stronger than among Hollywood actresses. In fact, Lawrence has been criticized in the press because she is not stick-thin—something that infuriates her.

In a 2013 interview with *Harper's Bazaar*, Lawrence recalled that when she was younger, film executives pressured her to lose weight. And because she was so young and impressionable, the experience was particularly painful, and she vows that she will never again let people do that to her. "Somebody told me I was fat, that I was going to get fired if I didn't lose a certain amount of weight. They brought in pictures of me where I was basically naked and told me to use them as motivation for my diet. It was just the kind of s- -t that actresses have to go through. . . . I was a little girl. I was hurt. It doesn't matter what accolades you get. I know it'll never happen to me again."[110]

Strong and Fit

When she was playing Mystique in *X-Men*, the thought struck her that she never wanted girls who would watch the movie to feel that same pressure about their weight:

> I remember thinking, "If I'm going to be naked in paint in front of the entire world, I'm going to look like a woman. I'm going to have curves and have boobs and have a butt. Because girls are going to look at that, and if I look like a scarecrow, they are going to think, "Oh, that's normal." It's not normal. I'm just so sick of these young girls with diets. I remember when I was 13 and it was cool to pretend to have an eating disorder because there were rumors that Lindsay Lohan and Nicole Richie were anorexic. I thought it was crazy. I went home and told my mom, "Nobody's eating bread—I just had to finish everyone's burgers." I think it's really important for girls to have people to look up to and to feel good about themselves.[111]

But Lawrence realizes that "fat shaming" continues to be very real, and many young women in and out of Hollywood are affected by it. And it is not only gossip columns and movie magazines that take shots at actresses who they think are not skinny enough. In fact, after Lawrence was chosen for the role of Katniss in *The Hunger Games*, the *New York Times* movie critic Manohla Dargis criticized her as too thick to play the role. Dargis wrote, "A few years ago Ms. Lawrence might have looked hungry enough to play Katniss, but now, at 21, her seductive, womanly figure makes a bad fit for a dystopian fantasy about a people starved into submission."[112]

Lawrence maintains that it would have made no sense for a successful hunter such as Katniss to look emaciated. "I don't want little girls to be like, 'Oh, I want to look like Katniss, so I'm going to skip dinner.' That's something that I was really conscious of during training, when you're trying to get your body to look exactly right. I was trying to get my body to look fit and strong—not thin and underfed."[113]

Jennifer Lawrence plays basketball in Los Angeles, California, in 2012. She has said she is proud not to fit in to the Hollywood stereotype of the rail-thin actress.

Many young women have applauded her comments as being realistic and helpful. Notes Brooklyn psychology student Grace Mathre:

It's refreshing to finally have positive role models for young girls, especially in a time where the media constantly attacks their self-esteem. Jennifer's advocacy isn't alone in Hollywood, but her personality definitely makes her more relatable. Body image is especially stressful throughout a girl's life, and for Jennifer to show them to love themselves and their bodies is fantastic. I mean, this is the woman who—when asked how she prepared for a role in a film—eats pizza while reading a script. This is the woman that photo-bombs other [celebrities'] red carpet photos. This is the woman that said, "We see this airbrushed perfect model . . . but you just have to look past it. . . . We [need to] stop treating each other like that, stop calling each other fat and stop with these unrealistic expectations for women. It's disappointing that the media keeps it alive and fuels that fire." How can you not love her?[114]

Changed by Success?

Those who know Jennifer Lawrence best—her friends and family—say that success, wealth, and fame have not changed who she is; but she is still criticized for being outspoken and not playing the "Hollywood game." Her assistant, Justine, who is also one of Lawrence's closest friends, explains:

It's because she's honest. It sounds a little cheesy, but she has a real person's body, she cusses and says the wrong things on television, and she's just herself. Literally everyone else is playing the game, but she is not. And I don't think she's capable of playing it, frankly. The number-one question I'm asked is "Has she changed?" And I get such pleasure in being able to say, "No. If anything, she's gotten more grounded, more normal."[115]

Jennifer Lawrence and her then boyfriend Nicholas Hoult visit the Formula One paddock in Monte Carlo, Monaco, in 2012. Friends and family say Jennifer has not let fame and wealth change her.

Of course, because Lawrence is young, it is realistic to assume that she will make mistakes along the way—and those things will be amplified. "It's hard because we don't feel any different," her family told a Louisville news outlet in 2013. "That's been the hardest part. She's a 22-year-old human being, and she will make the same mistakes we all make. . . . She's just going to make those mistakes under a microscope."[116]

In the meantime, however, whether playing Katniss, Mystique, or a new film character, Jennifer Lawrence will continue to entertain and move audiences with what have become her trademarks—style, humor, and candor.

Introduction: The Stumble Seen Around the World

1. YouTube. "Jennifer Lawrence Winning Best Actress," March 4, 2013. www.youtube.com/watch?v=WDU7 zLAd2-U.
2. YouTube. "Jennifer Lawrence Winning Best Actress."
3. YouTube. "Jennifer Lawrence Backstage After 2013 Oscar Win," March 4, 2013. www.youtube.com/watch?v=CLKZ b1wLmAY.
4. YouTube. "Jennifer Lawrence Backstage After 2013 Oscar Win."
5. YouTube. "Jennifer Lawrence Backstage After 2013 Oscar Win."
6. Jonathan Van Meter. "*The Hunger Games*' Jennifer Lawrence Covers the September Issue." *Vogue*, August 12, 2013. www.vogue.com/magazine/article/star-quality -jennifer-lawrence-hunger-games/#1.
7. Quoted in Jane Graham. "Jennifer Lawrence: A Shot of Kentucky Spirit." *The Guardian* (Manchester, UK), September 2, 2010. www.theguardian.com/film/2010/sep/02 /jennifer-lawrence-sitting-pretty.
8. Quoted in *Vanity Fair*. "Jennifer Lawrence on How Acting 'Is Stupid,' and the Time She Almost Shot Suspected Home Invaders with Her Bow and Arrow," January 2, 2013. www.vanityfair.com/online/oscars/2013/01/jennifer -lawrence-acting-stupid-bow.

Chapter 1: Growing Up Nitro

9. Quoted in Josh Eells. "Jennifer Lawrence: America's Kick-Ass Sweetheart." *Rolling Stone*, April 12, 2012. www .rollingstone.com/movies/news/jennifer-lawrence-ameri cas-kick-ass-sweetheart-20120412.
10. Quoted in Eells. "Jennifer Lawrence."

11. Quoted in Eells. "Jennifer Lawrence."
12. Quoted in Rachel Rosenblit. "Call of the Siren: Jennifer Lawrence." *Elle*, May 16, 2011. www.elle.com/pop-culture /celebrities/call-of-the-siren-jennifer-lawrence-562378.
13. Quoted in Van Meter. "*The Hunger Games*' Jennifer Lawrence Covers the September Issue."
14. Quoted in Maggie Bullock, "Jennifer Lawrence: Game Changer," *Elle*, December 2012, p. 304.
15. Quoted in Cassie Carpenter. "Before She Was Famous: School Pictures Reveal a Gawky 13-Year-Old Jennifer Lawrence with a Dodgy Perm." *Mail* Online, March 23, 2012. www.dailymail.co.uk/tvshowbiz/article-2119592 /Jennifer-Lawrence-pictured-aged-13-old-school-pictures -dodgy-perm.html.
16. *Saturday Night Live*. "Spartan Cheerleaders at a Chess Tournament," January 20, 1996. www.nbc.com/saturday -night-live/video/spartan-cheerleaders-at-a-chess-tourna ment/n10803.
17. Quoted in *Huffington Post*. "Jennifer Lawrence Reveals She Battled Anxiety Growing Up: 'I Felt Worthless,'" November 18, 2013. www.huffingtonpost.com/2013 /11/18/jennifer-lawrence-anxiety-battle_n_4296600.html.
18. Quoted in Van Meter. "*The Hunger Games*' Jennifer Lawrence Covers the September Issue."
19. Quoted in Van Meter. "*The Hunger Games*' Jennifer Lawrence Covers the September Issue."
20. Quoted in Van Meter. "*The Hunger Games*' Jennifer Lawrence Covers the September Issue."
21. Quoted in Johanna Schneller. "Thanks for Raising Me, but I'm Going to Take It from Here." *Globe and Mail* (Toronto), June 11, 2010. www.theglobeandmail.com/arts /film/interview-with-winters-bone-star-jennifer-lawrence /article4353312.
22. Quoted in Schneller. "Thanks for Raising Me."
23. Quoted in Josh Moss. "Too Young for Methods," February 9, 2011. www.louisville.com/content/too-young -methods-louisvilles-academy-award-nomianted-actress -jennifer-lawrence-movies.

24. Quoted in Eells. "Jennifer Lawrence."
25. Quoted in Moss. "Too Young for Methods."
26. Quoted in Iona Kirby and Hugo Daniel. "Fresh-Faced *Hunger Games* Star Jennifer Lawrence Pictured Before She Was Famous." *Mail* Online, March 27, 2012. www .dailymail.co.uk/tvshowbiz/article-2121264/Fresh-faced -Jennifer-Lawrence-pictured-famous--acting-coaches -praise-natural-talent.html.
27. Quoted in Moss. "Too Young for Methods."
28. Quoted in Elizabeth Woolsey. "Actress Jennifer Lawrence's Family Sits Down with WDRB." www.wdrb.com /story/21752231/actress-jennifer-lawrences-family-sits -down-with-wdrb.
29. Quoted in Schneller. "Thanks for Raising Me."
30. Quoted in Schneller. "Thanks for Raising Me."
31. Quoted in Eels. "Jennifer Lawrence."
32. Quoted in Moss. "Too Young for Methods."
33. Quoted in Van Meter. "*The Hunger Games'* Jennifer Lawrence Covers the September Issue."
34. Quoted in Shamecca Harris. "Jennifer Lawrence on Her Anxiety Disorder." ABC News blogs, November 18, 2013. https://gma.yahoo.com/blogs/abc-news/jennifer-lawrence -her-anxiety-disorder-203104323--abc-news-celebrities .html.

Chapter 2: Early Successes

35. Quoted in *Hollywood Reporter*. "Jennifer Lawrence's Career Journey, from 'Bill Engvall' to 'Hunger Games,'" March 22, 2012. www.hollywoodreporter.com/heat-vision /jennifer-lawrence-career-bill-engvall-winters-bone-hunger -games-303297.
36. Quoted in *Hollywood Reporter*. "Jennifer Lawrence's Career Journey."
37. Quoted in Sheila Roberts. "Interview: Jennifer Lawrence and Director Lori Petty on *The Poker House*." Collider, July 18, 2009. http://collider.com/interview-jennifer -lawrence-and-director-lori-petty-on-the-poker-house.
38. Quoted in Marlow Stern. "Lori Petty on 'Orange Is the

New Black,' the Halcyon 90s, and Discovering Jennifer Lawrence." *Daily Beast*, June 8, 2014. www.thedailybeast .com/articles/2014/06/08/lori-petty-on-orange-is-the-new -black-the-halcyon-90s-and-discovering-jennifer-lawrence .html.

39. Quoted in Stern. "Lori Petty on 'Orange Is the New Black.'"
40. Quoted in Stern. "Lori Petty on 'Orange Is the New Black.'"
41. Quoted in Roberts. "Interview."
42. Quoted in Roberts. "Interview."
43. Quoted in *Minding Therapy* (blog). "Two Oscar-Winning Actresses: Two Earlier Roles," February 27, 2013. www .mindingtherapy.com/oscar-winning-actresses-2.
44. Quoted in Jason Guerrasio. "Jennifer Lawrence Q & A." *Filmmaker*, February 26, 2011. http://filmmakermagazine .com/20347-jennifer-lawrence-qu/#.U71wQajlfwx.
45. Quoted in Steve Pond. "'Silver Linings' Oscar Nominee Jennifer Lawrence Shares Her Acting Secret: Never Sweat." The Wrap, February 15, 2013. www.thewrap.com/awards /column-post/silver-linings-playbook-oscar-nominee -jennifer-lawrence-shares-her-acting-secret-never-s.
46. Quoted in Schneller, "Thanks for Raising Me."
47. Quoted in Amanda Luttrell Garrigus. "Girl on Fire." *Flare*, June 2011, p. 128.
48. Quoted in Guerrasio. "Jennifer Lawrence Q & A."
49. Quoted in Reed Johnson. "Jennifer Lawrence, Play- ing to Strength." *Los Angeles Times*, November 11, 2010. http://articles.latimes.com/2010/nov/11/news/la-en-1111 -lawrence-20101111.
50. Quoted in Graham. "Jennifer Lawrence: A Shot of Ken- tucky Spirit."
51. Quoted in Graham. "Jennifer Lawrence: A Shot of Ken- tucky Spirit."
52. Quoted in Jerry Rice. "Lawrence Determined to the 'Bone.'" *Variety*, December 6, 2010. http://variety.com /2010/film/news/lawrence-determined-to-the-bone -1118028201.

53. Quoted in Moss. "Too Young for Methods."

Chapter 3: Jennifer's Big Break

54. Quoted in Guerrasio. "Jennifer Lawrence Q & A."
55. Quoted in Brad Balfour. "Best Actress Nominee Jennifer Lawrence Heats Up *Winter's Bone*." *Huffington Post*, February 25, 2011. www.huffingtonpost.com/brad-balfour/best-actress-jennifer- lawrence_b_828059.html.
56. Quoted in Kyle Buchanan. "The Verge: Jennifer Lawrence," *Movieline*, January 25, 2010. http://movieline.com/2010/01/25/the-verge-jennifer-lawrence.
57. Quoted in Guerrasio, "Jennifer Lawrence Q & A."
58. Quoted in Scott Feinberg. "Interview: Jennifer Lawrence, Star of 'Winter's Bone,' Next Big Thing," October 26, 2010. http://scottfeinberg.com/lawrenceinterview.
59. Quoted in Feinberg. "Interview: Jennifer Lawrence, Star of 'Winter's Bone.'"
60. Quoted in Graham. "Jennifer Lawrence: A Shot of Kentucky Spirit."
61. Quoted in Feinberg. "Interview: Jennifer Lawrence, Star of 'Winter's Bone.'"
62. Quoted in Johnson. "Jennifer Lawrence, Playing to Strength."
63. Quoted in Moss. "Too Young For Methods."
64. Quoted in Balfour. "Best Actress Nominee Jennifer Lawrence Heats Up *Winter's Bone*."
65. Quoted in Buchanan. "The Verge: Jennifer Lawrence."
66. Quoted in Jarett Wieselman, "Get to Know: Jennifer Lawrence," Page Six, June 17, 2010. http://pagesix.com/2010/06/17/get-to-know-jennifer-lawrence.
67. Quoted in Jay A. Fernandez, "Jennifer Lawrence: The Making of an 'It' Actress." *Hollywood Reporter*, January 19, 2011. www.hollywoodreporter.com/news/jennifer-lawrence-making-actress-72984.
68. A.O. Scott. "Where Life Is Cold and Kin Are Cruel," *New York Times*, June 10, 2010. www.nytimes.com/2010/06/11/movies/11winter.html?_r=0.
69. David Denby. "Thrills and Chills." *New Yorker*, July 5,

2010. www.newyorker.com/magazine/2010/07/05/thrills
-and-chills.

70. Quoted in Moss, "Too Young For Methods."
71. Quoted in Eells. "Jennifer Lawrence."
72. Quoted in Eells. "Jennifer Lawrence."
73. Quoted in Carina Adly MacKenzie. "'Hunger Games'
Star Jennifer Lawrence Eats Cheese Steak and She's Not
Afraid to Admit It," *zap2it* (blog), May 17, 2011. www
.zap2it.com/blogs/hunger_games_star_jennifer_lawrence
_eats_cheese_steak_and_shes_not_afraid_to_admit_it
-2011-05.
74. Quoted in Jen Chaney. "Louisville's Jennifer Lawrence
Can Barely Keep Up with Her Own Success." *Washington
Post*, June 3, 2011. www.kentucky.com/2011/06/03
/1760923/louisvilles-jennifer-lawrence.html.
75. Quoted in Joseph Lord. "Louisville's Jennifer Lawrence
Waits for Magical Oscar Nomination." *Louisville Courier-
Journal*, January 23, 2011. http://www.courier-journal.com
/apps/pbcs.dll/article?AID=/20110123/FEATURES07/3012
30059/&template=artiphone
76. Quoted in Elizabeth Woolsey. "Jennifer Lawrence's
Family Talks About Life in the Spotlight." WDRB.com,
March 20, 2013. www.wdrb.com/story/21759963/oscar
-winners-family-talks-about-life-with-jennifer-lawrence.

Chapter 4: Hungry for More

77. Quoted in Marlow Stern. "Jennifer Lawrence Is the
Breakout Star of *Winter's Bone!*" *Manhattan Movie Magazine*, June 12, 2010. www.manhattanmoviemag.com
/interviews/jennifer-lawrence-is-the-breakout-star-of
-winter%E2%80%99s-bone.html.
78. Quoted in Sheila. "*Hunger Games* Featured in 'Life
Story: Film Fantasy' Magazine." HG: Girl on Fire (*Hunger
Games* fansite), November 9, 2011. www.hggirlonfire.com
/2011/11/09/hunger-games-featured-in-life-story-film
-fantasy-magazine.
79. Quoted in Georgia Dehn. "*X-Men*: Jennifer Lawrence
Interview." *The Telegraph* (London), May 23, 2011. www

.telegraph.co.uk/culture/film/starsandstories/8526466/X
-Men-Jennifer-Lawrence-interview.html.

80. Quoted in Dehn. "*X-Men*: Jennifer Lawrence Interview."

81. Quoted in Jen Chaney. "Jennifer Lawrence Talks
'X-Men,' Fame, and 'Hunger Games.'" *Celebritology* (blog).
Washington Post.com, May 29, 2011. www.washingtonpost
.com/blogs/celebritology/post/jennifer-lawrence-talks-x
-men-fame-and-hunger-games/2011/05/29/AGqKrBEH
_blog.html.

82. Quoted in Dave McNary. "'Hunger Games': Can 'Catching Fire' Burn Brighter than the Original?" *Variety*, October 29, 2013. http://variety.com/2013/biz/news/hunger
-games-can-catching-fire-burn-brighter-than-the-original
-1200773163.

83. Quoted in Amy Longsdorf. "From Here to Panem."
LEO Weekly, March 27, 2012. http://leoweekly.com/ae
/here-panem.

84. Quoted in Longsdorf. "From Here to Panem."

85. Quoted in Longsdorf. "From Here to Panem."

86. Quoted in Bob Thompson. "*The Hunger Games*: Jennifer
Lawrence on Playing Katniss Everdeen." Postmedia News,
March 22, 2012. http://arts.nationalpost.com/2012/03/22
/the-hunger-games-jennifer-lawrence-i-think-im-as-ready
-as-i-can-be.

87. Quoted in Longsdorf. "From Here to Panem."

88. Quoted in Eells. "Jennifer Lawrence."

89. Quoted in Meriah Doty. "How Jennifer Lawrence Stole
Her 'Silver Linings Playbook' Role." *Movie Talk* (blog).
https://movies.yahoo.com/blogs/movie-talk/jennifer
-lawrence-stole-her-silver-linings-playbook-role-2331370
43.html.

90. Quoted in Eells. "Jennifer Lawrence."

91. Quoted in Eells. "Jennifer Lawrence."

Chapter 5: Oscar and Beyond

92. Quoted in Woolsey. "Actress Jennifer Lawrence's Family
Sits Down with WDRB."

93. Quoted in Eells. "Jennifer Lawrence."

94. Quoted in Schneller. "Thanks for Raising Me."

95. Quoted in Pond. "'Silver Linings' Oscar Nominee Jennifer Lawrence Shares Her Acting Secret."

96. Quoted in Pond. "'Silver Linings' Oscar Nominee Jennifer Lawrence Shares Her Acting Secret."

97. Quoted in Pond, "'Silver Linings' Oscar Nominee Jennifer Lawrence Shares Her Acting Secret."

98. Quoted in The Hunger Games Nation (fansite). "HQ Scans and Full Transcripts from the *Entertainment Weekly* Hunger Games' Issue, May 25, 2011. http://thehunger gamesnation.weebly.com/1/post/2011/05/hq-scans-full -transcript-from-the-entertainment-weekly-hunger-games -issue.html.

99. Quoted in The Hunger Games Nation. "HQ Scans and Full Transcripts."

100. Quoted in *Daily Mail* Reporter. "In Hollywood I'm Obese; I'm Considered a Fat Actress." *Daily Mail* (London), November 8, 2012. www.dailymail.co.uk/tvshow biz/article-2229927/Hunger-Games-star-Jennifer-Lawrence -says-shes-considered-obese-Hollywood-standards.html.

101. Quoted in Van Meter. "The Hunger Games' Jennifer Lawrence Covers the September Issue."

102. Quoted in Van Meter. "The Hunger Games' Jennifer Lawrence Covers the September Issue."

103. Quoted in Van Meter. "The Hunger Games' Jennifer Lawrence Covers the September Issue."

104. Quoted in Rotten Tomatoes. "American Hustle." www .rottentomatoes.com/m/american_hustle.

105. Quoted in Richard Roeper & the Movies. "American Hustle." www.richardroeper.com/reviews/americanhustle .aspx.

106. Quoted in *USA Today*. "'X-Men: Days of Future Past' Shows Humanity and Humor," May 22, 2014. www .usatoday.com/story/life/movies/2014/05/21/x-men-days -of-future-past-review/9392745.

107. Tom Riordan. Telephone interview with the author, July 14, 2014.

108. Quoted in Woolsey. "Jennifer Lawrence's Family Talks

About Life in the Spotlight."

109. Quoted in Woolsey. "Jennifer Lawrence's Family Talks About Life in the Spotlight."

110. Quoted in Chiderah Monde. "Jennifer Lawrence Recalls Being Called Fat." *New York Daily News*, October 2, 2013. www.nydailynews.com/entertainment/gossip/jennifer -lawrence-recalls-called-fat-article-1.1474067.

111. Quoted in Witty Profiles. "Jennifer Lawrence." www.wit typrofiles.com/q/6135616.

112. Quoted in L.V. Anderson. "Jennifer Lawrence Is Not 'Too Big' to Play Katniss." *Slate*, March 23, 2012. www .slate.com/blogs/browbeat/2012/03/23/jennifer_lawrence _s_body_not_skinny_enough_to_play_katniss_.html.

113. Quoted in Maggie Bullock. "Jennifer Lawrence: Game Changer." *Elle*, November 8, 2012, p. 304.

114. Gracie Mathre. Personal interview with the author, June 30, 2014, Minneapolis, MN.

115. Quoted in Van Meter. "'The Hunger Games' Jennifer Lawrence Covers the September Issue."

116. Quoted in Woolsey. "Actress Jennifer Lawrence's Family Sits Down With WDRB."

1990
Jennifer is born in Louisville, Kentucky, to Karen and Gary Lawrence.

2003
Lawrence is voted "Most Talkative" in seventh grade.

2004
Lawrence persuades her parents to take her to New York so she can attempt an acting or modeling career.

2006
Lawrence lands a small part in an episode of *Monk*.

2007
Lawrence joins the cast of *The Bill Engvall Show* on TBS, playing Engvall's daughter Lauren. She also wins roles in the independent films *The Poker House* and *The Burning Plain*.

2008
Lawrence and her family travel to Venice, Italy, where she wins the Marcello Mastroianni Award for Best New Young Actress for her work in *The Burning Plain*.

2009
Lawrence is cast as Ree Dolly in *Winter's Bone*.

2010
Lawrence's portrayal of Ree Dolly in *Winter's Bone* is praised by critics, and the film wins the Grand Jury Prize at the Sundance Film Festival in January.

2011
Lawrence is nominated for both an Academy Award and a Golden Globe Award for *Winter's Bone*; she is chosen to play Katniss Everdeen in *The Hunger Games*.

2012
Lawrence begins filming *The Hunger Games: Catching Fire*.

2013
Lawrence wins the Academy Award for Best Performance by an Actress in a Leading Role for *Silver Linings Playbook; The Hunger Games: Catching Fire* is released.

2014
Lawrence is nominated for an Oscar for Best Supporting Actress for her work in *American Hustle; X-Men: Days of Future Past* is released.

Books

Suzanne Collins. *The Hunger Games*. New York: Scholastic, 2008. The first book in the series of books made into films starring Jennifer Lawrence as Katniss Everdeen.

Melissa Higgins. *Jennifer Lawrence: Breakout Actress*. North Mankato, MN: Abdo, 2013. Fairly easy reading, with good photos and an interesting section on the making of some of her earliest movies, as well as the blockbusters, such as the *Hunger Games* and *X-Men* films.

Katherine Krohn. *Jennifer Lawrence: Star of the Hunger Games*. Minneapolis: Lerner, 2012. Excellent photographs, as well as good information on the hard work involved in filming *The Hunger Games*.

Mick O'Shea. *Beyond District 12: The Stars of* The Hunger Games: *Jennifer Lawrence, Josh Hutcherson, Liam Hemsworth*. London (UK): Plexus, 2012. This very readable book has a lot of good quotes from Lawrence, as well as from her co-stars.

Periodicals and Internet Sources

Simon Button. "Hunger Games Actress Jennifer Lawrence: I Changed Schools a Lot Because Girls Were Mean." *Daily Express* (UK), November 17, 2013. http://www.express.co.uk /entertainment/films/443460/Hunger-Games-actress-Jen nifer-Lawrence-I-changed-schools-a-lot-because-girls-were -mean. This article contains good quotes about Lawrence's early days looking for acting work.

Orlando Parfitt. "The Story Behind Amazing Footage of Jennifer Lawrence Comforting Crying Hunger Games Fan." Yahoo UK Movie News, November 12, 2013. A good article detailing Lawrence making time for a fan in a wheelchair.

A.O. Scott. "Where Life Is Cold and Kin Are Cruel." *New York Times*, June 10, 2010. http://www.nytimes.com/2010/06/11 /movies/11winter.html. An excellent review of *Winter's Bone*, the movie that pushed Lawrence into stardom.

Websites

The Hunger Games Wiki (http://thehungergames.wikia.com). This site is dedicated to the characters, the plots, and the universe of Suzanne Collins's books, although there are articles, reviews, and character sketches that pertain to the films. In addition, there are quizzes, photographs, and message boards for fans to chat.

Jennifer Lawrence.org (http://jenniferlawrence.org). This site includes information about Lawrence's movies, the roles she has played, thumbnail sketches of plots, and interesting quotations from her films. Primarily a fansite, it also keeps readers abreast of Lawrence's future projects.

Jennifer Lawrence Daily (http://jenniferlawrencedaily.com). Besides up-to-date news stories and biographical information about Jennifer Lawrence and her current and upcoming projects, there is a photo gallery, a collection of quotes, and facts about her life that fans will find interesting.

Picture Credits

Cover: © Dominique Charriau/WireImage/Getty Images

© 2929 Productions/Newscom, 35

© Albert L. Ortega/Getty Images, 12

© Alexandra Wyman/Getty Images for Grey Goose, 20

© Amy Graves/WireImage/Getty Images, 33

© AP Images/Carlo Allegri, 51

© AP Images/Charles Sykes, 79

© Dan MacMedan/WireImage/Getty Images, 56

© Didier Baverel/WireImage/Getty Images, 91

© Dominique Charriau/WireImage, 37

© face to face/Zuma Press/Newscom, 85

© Fayes Vision/WENN/Newscom, 29

© Gaz Shirley, PacificCoastNews/Newscom, 89

© GVK/Bauer Griffin/FilmMagic/Newscom, 81

© Icon Entertainment International/Newscom, 57

© Jason Merritt/Getty Images, 19

© Jeff Vespa/Getty Images, 74

© Kevin Winter/Getty Images, 6

© KPA/Zuma Press/Newscom, 40

© KRT/Newscom, 14

© Mirage Enterprises/Newscom, 73

© Murray Close/Getty Images, 62–63. 64

© Rex Features via AP Images, 67, 70

© Sebastian Mlynarski/UPI/Newscom, 48

© Splash News/Newscom, 11

© Very Productions/Newscom, 27

© Zuma Press/Newscom, 45, 53

Gail Stewart is the author of more than two hundred books for teens and young adults. She lives in Minneapolis with her husband and is the mother of three grown sons.